Essential

Greek
phrase book

PERIPLUS

First published in 2001 by Periplus Editions (HK) Ltd, with editorial offices at 153 Milk Street, Boston, Massachusetts 02109 and 5 Little Road #08-01, Singapore 536983

Library of Congress Cataloging-in-Publication Data

Library of Congress Catalog Card Number: 2001086472
ISBN: 962-593-928-8

Distributed by

USA
Tuttle Publishing
Distribution Center
Airport Industrial Park
364 Innovation Drive
North Clarendon, VT 05759-9436
Tel: (802) 773-8930
Toll free tel: (800) 526-2778
Fax: (802) 773-6993
Toll free fax: (800)329-8885

JAPAN
Tuttle Publishing
RK Building, 2nd Floor
2-13-10 Shimo-Meguro,
Meguro-Ku
Tokyo 153 0064
Tel: (03) 5437-0171
Fax: (03) 5437-0755

SOUTHEAST ASIA
Berkeley Books LTD
5 Little Road #08-01
Cemtex Industrial Bldg
Singapore 536983
Tel: (65) 280-1330
Fax: (65) 280-6290

First edition
07 06 05 04 03 02 01   10 9 8 7 6 5 4 3 2 1

Printed in Singapore

Contents

Introduction

● **Welcome to the Periplus new Essential Phrase Books series, covering the most popular European languages and containing everything you'd expect from a comprehensive language series. They're concise, accessible and easy to understand, and you'll find them indispensable on your trip abroad.**

Each guide is divided into 15 themed sections and starts with a pronunciation table which gives you the phonetic spelling to all the words and phrases you'll need to know for your trip, while at the back of the book is an extensive word list and grammar guide which will help you construct basic sentences in your chosen language.

Throughout the book you'll come across colored boxes with a 🌐 beside them. These are designed to help you if you can't understand what your listener is saying to you. Hand the book over to them and encourage them to point to the appropriate answer to the question you are asking.

Other colored boxes in the book—this time without the symbol—give alphabetical listings of themed words with their English translations beside them.

For extra clarity, we have put all English words and phrases in black, foreign language terms in red and their phonetic pronunciation in italic.

This phrase book covers all subjects you are likely to come across during the course of your visit, from reserving a room for the night to ordering food and drink at a restaurant and what to do if your car breaks down or you lose your traveler's checks and money. With over 2,000 commonly used words and essential phrases at your fingertips you can rest assured that you will be able to get by in all situations, so let the Essential Phrase Book become your passport to a secure and enjoyable trip!

Pronunciation table

The sounds of Greek are not particularly easy for an English speaker. In the pronunciation guide given for each word or phrase, the following system is used:

a	somewhere between English **a** in **car** and **u** in **cup**
b	similar to an English **b** but less aggressive
ch	as Scottish **ch** in **loch**
d	similar to an English **d** but less agressive
dh	as English **th** in **the**, **this**, **them**
e	as English **e** in **met**
f	as English **f** in **soft**
g	as English **g** in **go**
gh	a difficult sound: try saying a hard English **g** (as in **grab**) as far down your throat as possible.
h	a more breathy form of the English **h** in **hoot**
i	like the **ee** in **feet**, but make the sound more clipped
k	like the English **c** in **cat**
l	as English **l** in **lick**
m	as English **m** in **mat**
n	as English **n** in **not**
ng	just like the **ng** in **English**
o	like the English **o** in **pop**
oo	like the **oo** in English **ooze**
p	a lot less explosive than an English **p**
r	lightly rolled, as in Italian or Scottish: keep your tongue much closer to the back of your teeth than in a English **r**
s	as in English **sit**
t	more or less as in English **tap**
th	as English soft **th** in **thistle**
v	as in English **van**
w	as in English **went**
x	as the **x** in **box**
y	not a vowel but a glide, as in **yes**, **you**, **yacht**
z	as in English **zoo** or the **s** at the end of **was**

Note also the following combinations:

n(g)x	somewhere between English **things** and **thinks**
n(g)ch	as in the middle of **melancholy**

Stress and accents

In the pronunciation guide the stresses are marked with an accent, e.g. **o patéras** (father). The vowel **ou** is transcribed as **oo** when not stressed and **óo** when stressed. Any two other vowels together in the transcription must be pronounced separately, e.g. **aerodhrómyo** must be pronounced **a-e-rodhrómyo**, as must **oó**, which indicates two independent adjacent **o** sounds.

Useful lists

.1 Today or tomorrow?

What day is it today? _____ Τί μέρα είναι σήμερα;
Ti méra íne símera?

Today's Monday_____ Σήμερα είναι Δευτέρα
Símera íne dheftéra

– Tuesday_____ Σήμερα είναι Τρίτη
Símera íne tríti

– Wednesday _____ Σήμερα είναι Τετάρτη
Símera íne tetárti

– Thursday_____ Σήμερα είναι Πέμπτη
Símera íne pémpti

– Friday_____ Σήμερα είναι Παρασκευή
Símera íne paraskeví

– Saturday _____ Σήμερα είναι Σάββατο
Símera íne sávato

– Sunday _____ Σήμερα είναι Κυριακή
Símera íne kiriakí

in January _____ τον Ιανουάριο
ton yanooário

since February _____ από το Φεβρουάριο
apó to fevrooário

in spring_____ την άνοιξη
tin ánixi

in summer_____ το καλοκαίρι
to kalokyéri

in autumn _____ το φθινόπωρο
to fthinóporo

in winter_____ το χειμώνα
to himóna

2001_____ δύο χιλιάδες ένα
dhío hilyádhes éna

the twentieth century _____ τον εικοστό αιώνα
ton ikostó eóna

What's the date today? ____ Τί ημερομηνία έχουμε σήμερα/Πόσες του μηνός έχουμε σήμερα;
ti imerominía éhome símera/póses too minós éhome símera?

Today's the 24th_____ Σήμερα είναι 24 του μηνός
símera íne ikositéseres too minós

Monday 5 November _____ Δευτέρα, 5 Νοεμβρίου 2001
2001 *dheftéra pénde noemvríoo dhío hilyádhes éna*

in the morning _____ το πρωί
to proí

in the afternoon _____ το μεσημέρι
to mesiméri

in the evening _____ το βράδυ
to vrádhi

at night_____ τη νύχτα
ti níchta

this morning _____ σήμερα το πρωί
símera to proí

this afternoon _____	σήμερα το μεσημέρι
	símera to mesiméri
this evening _____	σήμερα το απόγευμα
	símera to apóyevma
tonight _____	απόψε
	apópse
last night _____	την περασμένη νύχτα
	timberasméni níchta
this week _____	αυτή την εβδομάδα
	avtí tin evdhomádha
next month _____	τον επόμενο μήνα
	ton epómeno mína
last year _____	πέρυσι
	périsi
next... _____	τον επόμενο.../την επόμενη.../το επόμενο...
	ton epómeno.../tin epómeni.../to epómeno...
in...days/weeks/ _____ months/years	σε...μέρες/εβδομάδες/μήνες/χρόνια
	se...méres/evdhomádhes/hrónia
...weeks ago _____	πριν από... εβδομάδες
	prin apó...evdhomádhes
day off _____	αργία
	aryía

 .2 Legal holidays

● **The most important** public holidays in Greece are the following:

January 1	(New Year's Day) Η Πρωτοχρονιά
January 6	(Epiphany) Τα Επιφάνια
March 25	(The anniversary of the start of the War of Independence against the Turks in 1826) Εικοστή Πέμπτη Ιουλίου
April/May	(Easter: Greek Easter is celebrated according to the Orthodox Church calendar, and occurs on different dates from American Easter) Πάσχα
May 1	(May Day, Labor Day) Πρωτομαγιά
May/June	(Ascension; Pentecost) Της Αναλήψεως
August 15	(Assumption) Η Κοίμησις της Θεοτόκου
October 28	("No! Day": the day on which the Greeks refused the Italian ultimatum in 1940) Εικοστή Ογδόη Οκτωβρίου
December 25	(Christmas) Χριστούγεννα

Most shops, banks and government institutions are closed on these days. Good Friday and December 26 are not holidays.

.3 What time is it?

What time is it? _____	Τί ώρα είναι;
	ti óra íne?
It's nine o'clock _____	Είναι εννιά
	íne enyá
– five past ten _____	Είναι δέκα και πέντε
	íne dhéka ke pénde
– a quarter past eleven ____	Είναι έντεκα και τέταρτο
	íne éndeka ke tétarto
– twenty past twelve_____	Είναι δώδεκα και είκοσι
	íne dhódheka ke íkosi

– half past one _____ Είναι μιάμιση
íne myámisi

– twenty–five to three_____ Είναι τρεις παρά είκοσι πέντε
íne tris pará íkosi pénde

– a quarter to four _____ Είναι τέσσερες παρά τέταρτο
íne téseres pará tétarto

– ten to five _____ Είναι πέντε παρά δέκα
íne pénde pará dhéka

– twelve noon _____ Είναι δώδεκα το μεσημέρι
íne dhódheka to mesiméri

– midnight _____ Είναι μεσάνυχτα
íne mesánichta

half an hour _____ μισή ώρα
misí óra

What time? _____ Τι ώρα;
ti óra?

What time can I come _____ Τι ώρα μπορώ να περάσω;
  round? *ti óra boró na peráso?*

At... _____ Στις...
stis...

After... _____ Μετά τις...
metá tis...

Before... _____ Πριν από τις...
prin apó tis...

Between...and... _____ Μεταξύ...και...
metaxí... ke...

From...to... _____ Από τις...μέχρι τις...
apó tis... méhri tis...

In...minutes _____ Σε...λεπτά
se...leptá

– ...hours _____ Σε...ώρες
se...óres

– a quarter of an hour _____ Σ' ένα τέταρτο
s' éna tétarto

– three quarters of_____ Σε τρία τέταρτα
  an hour *se tría tétarta*

early _____ πολύ νωρίς
polí norís

on time _____ στην ώρα
stin óra

summertime _____ θερινή ώρα
theriní óra

wintertime _____ χειμερινή ώρα
himeriní óra

.4 One, two, three...

zero _____	μηδέν	*midhén*
1 _____	ένα	*éna*
2 _____	δύο	*dhío*
3 _____	τρία	*tría*
4 _____	τέσσερα	*téssera*
5 _____	πέντε	*pénde*
6 _____	έξι	*éxi*
7 _____	εφτά	*eftá*
8 _____	οχτώ	*ochtó*
9 _____	εννιά	*enyá*

10 _____	δέκα	*dhéka*
11 _____	ένδεκα	*éndheka*
12 _____	δώδεκα	*dhódheka*
13 _____	δεκατρία	*dhekatría*
14 _____	δεκατέσσερα	*dhekatésera*
15 _____	δεκαπέντε	*dhekapénde*
16 _____	δεκαέξι	*dhekaéxi*
17 _____	δεκαεφτά	*dhekaeftá*
18 _____	δεκαοχτό	*dhekaochtó*
19 _____	δεκαεννιά	*dekhaenyá*
20 _____	είκοσι	*íkosi*
21 _____	είκοσι ένα	*kosi éna*
22 _____	είκοσι δύο	*íkosi dhío*
30 _____	τριάντα	*triánda*
31 _____	τριάντα ένα	*triánda éna*
32 _____	τριάντα δύο	*triánda dhío*
40 _____	σαράντα	*saránda*
50 _____	πενήντα	*penínda*
60 _____	εξήντα	*exínda*
70 _____	εβδομήντα	*evdhomínda*
80 _____	ογδόντα	*oghdhónda*
90 _____	εννενήντα	*enenínda*
100 _____	εκατό	*ekató*
101 _____	εκατόν ένα	*ekatón éna*
110 _____	εκατό δέκα	*ekató dhéka*
120 _____	εκατόν είκοσι	*ekatón íkosi*
200 _____	διακόσια	*dhiakósia*
300 _____	τριακόσια	*triakósia*
400 _____	τετρακόσια	*tetrakósia*
500 _____	πεντακόσια	*pendakósia*
600 _____	εξακόσια	*exakósia*
700 _____	εφτακόσια	*eftakósia*
800 _____	οχτακόσια	*ochtakósia*
900 _____	εννιακόσια	*enyakósia*
1000 _____	χίλια	*hílya*
1100 _____	χίλια εκατό	*hílya ekató*
2000 _____	δύο χιλιάδες	*dhío hilyádhes*
10,000 _____	δέκα χιλιάδες	*dhéka hilyádhes*
100,000 _____	εκατό χιλιάδες	*ekató hilyádhes*
1,000,000 _____	ένα εκατομμύριο	*éna ekatomírio*
1st _____	πρώτος	*prótos*
2nd _____	δεύτερος	*dhéfteros*
3rd _____	τρίτος	*trítos*
4th _____	τέταρτος	*tétartos*
5th _____	πέμπτος	*pémptos*
6th _____	έκτος	*éktos*
7th _____	έβδομος	*évdhomos*
8th _____	όγδοος	*óghdhoos*
9th _____	ένατος	*énatos*
10th _____	δέκατος	*dhékatos*
11th _____	ενδέκατος	*endhékatos*
12th _____	δωδέκατος	*dhodhékatos*

13th	δέκατος τρίτος	*dhékatos trítos*
14th	δέκατος τέταρτος	*dhékatos tétartos*
15th	δέκατος πέμπτος	*dhékatos pémptos*
16th	δέκατος έκτος	*dhékatos éktos*
17th	δέκατος έβδομος	*dhékatos évdhomos*
18th	δέκατος όγδοος	*dhékatos óghdhoos*
19th	δέκατος ένατος	*dhékatos énatos*
20th	εικοστός	*ikostós*
21st	εικοστός πρώτος	*kostós prótos*
22nd	εικοστός δεύτερος	*ikostós dhéfteros*
30th	τριαντακοστός	*triandakostós*
100th	εκατοστός	*ekatostós*
1000th	χιλιοστός	*hilyostós*

once	μία φορά	*mía forá*
twice	δύο φορές	*dhío forés*
double	το διπλό	*to dhipló*
triple	το τριπλάσιο	*to triplásio*
half	το μισό	*to misó*
a quarter	ένα τέταρτο	*éna tétarto*
a third	ένα τρίτο	*éna tríto*
a few, some	μερικά	*meriká*

2+4=6	δύο και τέσσερα ίσον έξι	*dhío ke tésera íson éxi*
4-2=2	τέσσερα μείον δύο ίσον δύο	*tésera míon dhío íson dhío*
2x4=8	δύο επί τέσσερα ίσον οχτώ	*dhío epí tésera íson ochtó*
4÷2=2	τέσσερα διά δύο ίσον δύο	*tésera dhía dhío íson dhío*
odd/even	μονός/ζυγός	*mónos/zighós*
total	συνολικά	*sinoliká*
6x9	έξι επί εννιά	*éxi epí enyá*

🔵 *1*.5 The weather

Is the weather going to be good/bad?	Θα έχουμε καλό/κακό καιρό; *tha éhoome kaló/kakó kyeró?*
Is it going to get colder/hotter?	Θα κάνει περισσότερο κρύο/περισσότερη ζέστη; *tha káni perisótero krío/perisóteri zésti?*
What temperature is it going to be?	Τι θερμοκρασία θα κάνει σήμερα; *ti thermokrasía tha káni símera?*
Is it going to rain?	Θα βρέξει; *tha vréxi?*

Is there going to be a _____ storm?	Θα έχουμε θύελλα; *tha éhoome thíela?*
Is it going to snow? _____	Θα χιονίσει; *tha hyonísi?*
Is it going to freeze? _____	Θα κάνει παγωνιά; *tha káni pagonyá?*
Is the thaw setting in? _____	Θα λιώσουν τα χιόνια; *tha lyósoon ta hyónya?*
Is it going to be foggy? _____	Θα πέσει ομίχλη; *tha pési omíchli?*
Is there going to be a _____ thunderstorm?	Θα έχουμε καταιγίδα; *tha éhoome kateyídha?*
The weather's changing _____	Αλλάζει ο καιρός *alázi o kyerós*
It's cooling down _____	Δροσίζει *dhrosízi*
What's the weather _____ going to be like today/ tomorrow?	Τι καιρό θα έχουμε σήμερα/αύριο; *ti kyéro tha éhoome símera/ávrio?*

 .6 Here, there...

See also 5.1 Asking for directions

here/there _____	εδώ/εκεί *edhó/ekí*
somewhere/nowhere _____	κάπου/πουθενά *kápoo/poothená*
everywhere _____	παντού *pandóo*
far away/nearby _____	μακριά/κοντά *makriá/kondá*
to the right/left _____	προς τα δεξιά/αριστερά *pros ta dhexyá/aristerá*
on the right/left of _____	δεξιά/αριστερά από *dhexyá/aristerá apó*
straight ahead _____	ίσια *ísya*
via _____	μέσω *méso*
in _____	σε *se*
on _____	πάνω σε *páno se*
under _____	κάτω από *káto apó*
against _____	εναντίον *enandíon*
opposite _____	απέναντι *apénandi*
next to/near _____	δίπλα σε/κοντά σε *dhípla se/kondá se*
in front of _____	μπροστά *brostá*
in the center _____	στη μέση *sti mési*

άνεμος	ελαφρές νεφώσεις	ομίχλη
wind	**light cloud**	**mist/fog**
ανέφελος	ζεστός	παγετός
cloudless	**hot**	**frost**
αποπνικτικός	ηλιόλουστο	ριπέςαέρα
muggy/	**sunny**	**gusts of wind**
oppressive	θύελλα	συννεφιά
αφόρητη ζέστη	**storm**	**cloudy**
unbearable heat	καλός	τσουχτερός
...βαθμοί κάτω/πάνω	**fine**	**bitingly**
από το μηδέν	καύσωνας	**cold**
...degrees	**heatwave**	τυφώνας
below/above	μαλακός/ήπιος	**cyclone**
zero	**mild**	φυσάει
βαριές νεφώσεις	μέτριος/δυνατός	**it is windy**
heavy cloud	άνεμος	χαλάζι
βροχερός	**medium/strong**	**hail**
damp	**winds**	χιόνι
βροχή	μισοσυννεφιασμένος	**snow**
rain	**partly cloudy**	ψυχρός
δροσερός	μπόρα	**very cold**
cool	**squall of rain**	

forward_____	εμπρός/προς τα εμπρός	
	embrós/pros ta embrós	
down_____	(προς τα) κάτω	
	(pros ta) káto	
up_____	(προς τα) πάνω	
	(pros ta) páno	
inside _____	(προς τα) μέσα	
	(pros ta) mésa	
outside _____	(προς τα) έξω	
	(pros ta) éxo	
behind _____	(προς τα) πίσω	
	(pros ta) píso	
at the front _____	μπροστά	
	brostá	
at the back_____	πίσω - πίσω	
	píso-píso	
in the north _____	στο βορρά	
	sto vorá	
to the south_____	προς το νότο	
	pros to nóto	
from the west_____	από τη δύση	
	apó ti dhísi	
from the east _____	της ανατολής	
	tis anatolís	
north/south/west/east of ___	βόρεια/νότια/δυτικά/	
	ανατολικά από	
	vórya/nótya/dhitiká/	
	anatolitiká apó	

.7 What does that sign say?

See also 5.4 Traffic signs.

ΑΝΔΡΩΝ
gentlemen
ΑΝΕΛΚΥΣΤΗΡΑΣ
elevator
ΑΝΟΙΧΤΟ/ΚΛΕΙΣΤΟ
open/shut
ΑΠΑΓΟΡΕΥΕΤΑΙ Η
ΕΙΣΟΔΟΣ
no entry
ΑΠΑΓΟΡΕΥΕΤΑΙ Η
ΦΩΤΟΓΡΑΦΗΣΗ
no photography
ΑΠΑΓΟΡΕΥΕΤΑΙ ΝΑ
ΠΑΤΑΤΕ ΣΤΟ
ΓΡΑΣΙΔΙ
do not walk on the
grass
ΑΠΑΓΟΡΕΥΕΤΑΙ ΤΟ
ΚΑΠΝΙΣΜΑ
no smoking
ΑΠΑΓΟΡΕΥΟΝΤΑΙ ΤΑ
ΚΑΤΟΙΚΙΔΙΑ ΖΩΑ
no pets
ΑΠΟΧΩΡΗΤΗΡΙΑ/
ΤΟΥΑΛΕΤΤΕΣ
lavatories/toilets
ΓΥΝΑΙΚΩΝ
ladies
ΕΔΩ
ΠΛΗΡΟΦΟΡΙΕΣ
information desk
ΕΙΣΟΔΟΣ
entrance
ΕΚΠΤΩΣΕΙΣ
reduction/sale
ΕΚΤΟΣ ΛΕΙΤΟΥΡΓΙΑΣ
out of order

ΕΛΕΥΘΕΡΗ
ΕΙΣΟΔΟΣ
free entry
ΕΝΟΙΚΙΑΖΕΤΑΙ
to let
ΕΞΟΔΟΣ
exit
ΕΞΟΔΟΣ ΚΙΝΔΥΝΟΥ
emergency exit
ΙΔΙΟΚΤΗΣΙΑ
private/private
property
ΚΙΝΔΥΝΟΣ
danger
ΚΙΝΔΥΝΟΣ ΘΑΝΑΤΟΥ
danger!
ΚΙΝΔΥΝΟΣ
ΠΥΡΚΑΓΙΑΣ
fire hasard
ΚΛΕΙΣΜΕΝΟ/
ΡΕΖΕΡΒΕ
booked/reserved
ΚΥΛΙΟΜΕΝΗ
ΣΚΑΛΑ
escalator
ΜΗ ΠΟΣΙΜΟ ΝΕΡΟ
not drinking water
ΜΗΝ ΑΓΓΙΖΕΤΕ
do not touch
ΜΗΝ ΕΝΟΧΛΕΙΤΕ
do not disturb
ΟΡΟΦΟΣ
floor
ΠΛΗΡΕΣ
full
ΠΛΗΡΟΦΟΡΙΕΣ
information

ΠΡΟΣΟΧΗ ΒΑΦΗ
wet paint
ΠΡΟΣΟΧΗ ΣΚΥΛΟΣ
beware of the dog
ΠΡΟΣΟΧΗ ΤΟ
ΣΚΑΛΙ
watch your step
ΠΡΩΤΕΣ ΒΟΗΘΕΙΕΣ
accident and
emergency service
ΠΩΛΕΙΤΑΙ
for sale
ΡΕΣΕΨΙΟΝ
reception
ΣΗΜΑ ΚΙΝΔΥΝΟΥ
emergency
cord/alarm button
ΣΚΑΛΑ
stairs
ΣΚΑΛΑ ΠΥΡΚΑΓΙΑΣ
fire escape
ΣΥΡΑΤΕ/ΩΘΗΣΑΤΕ
pull/push
ΤΑΜΕΙΟ
cash desk/booking
office
ΥΓΡΟ
damp
ΥΨΗΛΗ ΤΑΣΙΣ
high tension
cables/high
voltage
ΞΕΠΟΥΛΗΜΑ
clearance sale
ΩΡΕΣ
ΛΕΙΤΟΥΡΓΙΑΣ
opening hours

.8 Telephone alphabet

α	_____	álfa	Αλέξανδρος	Aléxandhros
β	_____	víta	Βασίλιος	Vasílyos
γ	_____	gháma	Γεώργιος	Yéoryos
δ	_____	dhélta	Δημήτριος	Dhimítrios
ε	_____	épsilon	Ελένη	Eléni
ζ	_____	zíta	Ζωή	Zoí

η_____	íta	Ηρακλής	*Iraklís*
θ_____	thíta	Θεόδωρος	*Theódhoros*
ι_____	yóta	Ιωάννης	*Yoánis*
κ_____	kápa	Κωνσταντίνος	*Konstandínos*
λ_____	lámdha	Λεωνίδας	*Leonídhas*
μ_____	mi	Μενέλαος	*Menélaos*
ν_____	ni	Νικόλαος	*Nikólaos*
ξ_____	xi	Ξενοφών	*Xenofón*
ο_____	ómikron	Οδυσσέας	*Odhiséas*
π_____	pi	Περικλής	*Periklís*
ρ_____	ro	Ρόδος	*Ródhos*
σ_____	síghma	Σωτήριος	*Sotiríos*
τ_____	taf	Τιμολέων	*Timoléon*
υ_____	ípsilon	Υψηλάντης	*Ipsilándis*
φ_____	fi	Φώτιος	*Fótyos*
χ_____	hi	Χρήστος	*Chrístos*
ψ_____	psi	Ψάλτης	*Psáltis*
ω_____	omégha	Ωμέγα	*Omégha*

1 .9 Personal details

surname_____ επώνυμο
epónimo
christian/given name(s) ____ (μικρό) όνομα
(mikró) ónoma
initials_____ τα αρχικά
ta arhiká
address (street/number) ___ η διεύθυνση (οδός / αριθμός)
dhiéfthinsi (odhós/arithmós)
postal/zip code/town _____ ταχυδρομικός κώδικας / αριθμός κατοικίας
tahidhromikós kódikas/tópos katikías
sex (male/female) _____ φύλο (άρρεν / θήλυ)
fílo (áren/thíli)
nationality _____ υπηκοότητα
ipikoótita
date of birth _____ ημερομηνία γεννήσεως
imerominía yeníseos
place of birth _____ τόπος γεννήσεως
tópos yeníseos

16

occupation _____	επάγγελμα
	epàngelma
married/single/divorced ____	έγγαμος / άγαμος / διεζευγμένος
	éngamos/àgamos/dhiezevgménos
widowed _____	εν χηρεία
	en hiría
(number of) children _____	τέκνα (αριθμός τέκνων)
	tékna (arithmós téknon)
passport/identity _____	αριθμός ταυτότητας διαβατηρίου / άδειας
card/driving license	οδηγήσεως
number	*arithmós taftótitas dhiavatíryoo/ádhias*
	odhiyíseos
place and date of issue ____	τόπος και ημερομηνία έκδοσης
	tópos ke imerominía ékdhosis

Courtesies

 # **C**ourtesies

● **It is usual in Greece** for friends and relatives of both sexes to kiss each other on both cheeks when meeting and parting company. People who know each other less well shake hands instead.

.1 **G**reetings

Hello, Mr Smith _____	Γειά σας κύριε Σμιθ
	ya sas kírie Smith
Hello, Mrs Jones _____	Γειά σας κυρία Ντζωνς
	Ya sas kiría Jones
Hello, Peter _____	Γειά σου Πέτρο
	ya soo Pétro
Hi, Helen _____	Γειά σου Ελένη
	ya soo Eléni
Good morning, madam____	Καλημέρα κυρία
	kaliméra kiría
Good afternoon, sir _____	Καλησπέρα κύριε
	kalispéra kírie
Good evening_____	Καλησπέρα
	kalispéra
How are you? _____	Καλημέρα
	kaliméra
Fine, thank you, and you?__	Τί κάνετε;
	ti kánete
Very well _____	Καλά, κι εσείς;
	kalá kyesís?
Not very well _____	Πολύ καλά
	polí kalá
Not too bad_____	Οχι και τόσο καλά
	óhi ke tóso kalá
I'd better be going_____	Ετσι κι έτσι...
	étsi kyétsi
I have to be going _____	Φεύγω τώρα
	févgo tóra
Someone's waiting _____ for me. Bye!	Πρέπει να φύγω τώρα. Με περιμένουν
	prépi na fígo tóra. Me periménoon
Good-bye_____	Γεια σας !
	Ya sas!
See you soon _____	Αντίο
	adío
See you later _____	Θα σε δω αργότερα
	tha se dho argótera
See you in a little while ___	Θα σε δω σε λίγο
	tha se dho se lígho
Sleep well _____	Καληνύχτα
	kaliníchta
Good night _____	Καλό ύπνο
	kaló ípno
All the best _____	Στο καλό να πας/όλα καλά
	sto kaló na pas/ óla kalá
Have fun_____	Καλή διασκέδαση
	kalí dhiaskédhasi
Good luck _____	Καλή επιτυχία
	kalí epitihía

Have a nice vacation _____	Καλές διακοπές
	kalés dhiakopés
Have a good trip _____	Καλό ταξίδι
	kaló taxdíhi
Thank you, you too_____	Ευχαριστώ, επίσης
	efharistó, epísis
Say hello to...for me_____	Χαιρετισμούς σε...
	heretizmóos se...

.2 How to ask a question

Who?_____	Ποιός
	pyós?
Who's that? _____	Ποιός είναι;
	pyós íne?
What? _____	Τί;
	ti?
What's there to_____ see here?	Τί αξιοθέατα έχει εδώ; *ti axiothéata éhi edhó?*
What kind of hotel_____ is that?	Τί είδος ξενοδοχείο είναι αυτό; *ti ídhos xenodhohío íne aftó?*
What time is it? _____	Τί ώρα είναι;
	ti óra íne?
Where? _____	Πού;
	poo?
Where's the bathroom? ____	Πού είναι η τουαλέτα;
	poo íne i twaléta?
Where are you going? _____	Πού πηγαίνετε;
	poo piyénete?
Where are you from?_____	Από πού έρχεσθε;
	apó poo érhesthe?
How?_____	Πώς;
	pos?
How far is that? _____	Πόσο μακριά είναι;
	póso makriá íne?
How long does that take? __	Πόση ώρα διαρκεί/κρατάει; *pósi óra dhiarkí/kratái?*
How long is the trip? _____	Πόσο κρατάει το ταξίδι; *póso kratái to taxídhi?*
How much?_____	Πόσος;
	pósos
How much is this?_____	Πόσο κάνει;
	póso káni?
Which? _____	Ποιό; Ποιά;
	pyo? pya?
Which glass is mine? _____	Ποιό ποτήρι είναι δικό μου; *pyo potíri íne dhikó moo?*
When? _____	Πότε;
	póte?
When are you leaving? ____	Πότε φεύγετε;
	póte févyete?
Why?_____	Γιατί;
	yatí?
Could you...me?_____	Μπορείτε να με... ;
	boríte na me...?
Could you help me, _____ please?	Μπορείτε να με βοηθήσετε, παρακαλώ; *boríte na me voithísete, parakaló?*

Could you point that _____ out to me?	Μπορείτε να μου το δείξετε; *boríte na moo to dhíxete?*
Could you come _____ with me, please?	Μπορείτε να 'ρθείτε μαζί μου, παρακαλώ; *boríte narthíte mazí moo, parakaló?*
Could you... _____	Θέλετε...;/Μπορείτε... ; *thélete...?/Boríte...?*
Could you reserve some ___ tickets for me, please?	Μπορείτε να μου κλείσετε εισιτήρια, παρακαλώ; *boríte na moo klísete isitíria parakaló?*
Do you know...? _____	Ξέρετε...; *xérete...?*
Do you know another _____ hotel, please?	Μήπως ξέρετε κανένα άλλο ξενοδοχείο; *mípos xérete kanéna álo xenodhohío*
Do you know whether...? ___	Μήπως έχετε...; *mípos éhete...?*
Do you have a...? _____	Μπορείτε να μου δώσετε ένα...; *boríte na moo dhósete éna...?*
Do you have a _____ vegetarian dish, please?	Μήπως έχετε φαγητό χωρίς κρέας; *mípos éhete faitó chorís kréas?*
I'd like... _____	Θα ήθελα... *tha íthela...*
I'd like a kilo of apples, ___ please.	Θα ήθελα ένα κιλό μήλα *tha íthela éna kiló míla*
Can I...? _____	Μπορώ... ; *boró...?*
Can I take this? _____	Μπορώ να το πάρω μαζί μου; *boró na to páro mazí moo?*
Can I smoke here? _____	Μπορώ να καπνίσω εδώ; *boró na kapníso edhó?*
Could I ask you _____ something?	Μπορώ να ρωτήσω κάτι; *boró na rotíso káti?*

.3 How to reply

Yes, of course _____	Ναι, βέβαια/Βεβαίως *ne, vévea/vevéos*
No, I'm sorry _____	Όχι, λυπάμαι *óhi, lipáme*
Yes, what can I do _____ for you?	Ορίστε *oríste*
Just a moment, please ___	Μια στιγμή/Ένα λεπτό, παρακαλώ *mya stighmí/éna leptó parakaló*
No, I don't have _____ time now	Όχι, δε με βολεύει τώρα *óhi dhen me volévi tóra*
No, that's impossible _____	Όχι, δε γίνεται *óhi, dhe yínete*
I think so _____	Νομίζω *nomízo*
I agree _____	Κι εγώ το νομίζω *kyeghó to nomízo*
I hope so too _____	Κι εγώ το ελπίζω *kyeghó to elpízo*
No, not at all _____	Όχι, καθόλου *óhi kathóloo*
No, no one _____	Όχι, κανένας *óhi kanénas*

No, nothing _____ Οχι, τίποτα
óhi típota

That's (not) right _____ Ετσι είναι / (Δεν) είναι έτσι
étsi íne/(dhen) íne étsi

I (don't) agree _____ (Δε) συμφωνώ μαζί σας
(dhe) simfonó mazí sas

All right _____ Καλά
kalá

Okay _____ Εντάξει
endáxi

Perhaps _____ Ισως/Μπορεί
ísos/borí

I don't know _____ Δεν ξέρω
dhen xéro

.4 Thank you

Thank you _____ Ευχαριστώ
efcharistó

You're welcome _____ Παρακαλώ
parakaló

Thank you very much _____ Ευχαριστώ πολύ
efcharistó polí

Very kind of you _____ Πολύ ευγενικό εκ μέρους σας
polí evyenikó ek méroos sas

I enjoyed it very much_____ Χάρηκα πολύ
chárika polí

Thank you for your_____ Ευχαριστώ για τον κόπο
  trouble *efcharistó ya tongópo*

You shouldn't have _____ Δεν ήταν ανάγκη
dhen ítan anángi

That's all right _____ Δεν πειράζει
dhembirázi

.5 Sorry

Sorry! _____ Συγγνώμη
sighnómi

Excuse me_____ Με συγχωρείτε
me sinchoríte

I'm sorry, I didn't know...___ Συγγνώμη, δεν ήξερα ότι...
sighnómi dhen íxera óti...

I do apologize_____ Με συγχωρείτε
me sinchoríte

I'm sorry _____ Λυπάμαι
lipáme

I didn't do it on purpose,___ Δεν το 'κανα επίτηδες, έγινε κατά λάθος
  it was an accident *dhen tókana epítidhes, éyine katá láthos*

Never mind_____ Εντάξει έτσι
endáxi étsi

It could've happened to____ Αυτό μπορεί να συμβεί στον καθένα
  anyone *aftó borí na simví stongathéna*

.6 What do you think?

Which do you prefer?_____	Τί προτιμάτε; *ti protimáte?*
Do you like it?_____	Σου αρέσει; *soo arési?*
Don't you like dancing? ___	Δε σ' αρέσει να χορεύεις; *dhe sarési na chorévis?*
I don't mind _____	Το ίδιο μου κάνει *to ídhyo moo káni*
Well done! _____	Μπράβο! *brávo*
Not bad!_____	Οχι άσχημο! *óhi áschimo!*
Great! _____	Υπέροχο! *ipérocho!*
Wonderful! _____	θαυμάσιο! *thavmásio!*
It's really nice here! _____	Τι ωραία που είναι εδώ! *ti oréa poo íne edhó!*
How nice! _____	Τι ωραίο! *ti oréo!*
How nice for you! _____	Χαίρομαι για σας! *hérome ya sas!*
I'm (not) very _____ happy with...	(Δεν) είμαι πολύ ευχαριστημένος/ ευχαριστημένη με... *(dhen) íme polí efcharistiménos/ efcharistiméni me...*
I'm glad that... _____	Χαίρομαι που... *hérome poo ...*
I'm having a great time ____	Περνάω μια χαρά *pernáo mya chará*
I'm looking forward to it ___	Περιμένω ανυπόμονα *periméno anipómona*
I hope it'll work out_____	Ελπίζω να πετύχει *elpízo na petíhi*
What a mess! _____	Τί χάλια! *ti hálya!*
That's terrible! _____	Τί απαίσιο! *ti apésyo!*
What a pity! _____	Τί κρίμα! *ti kríma!*
That's filthy! _____	Τί αηδία! *ti aidhía!*
What nonsense!_____	Τί ανοησίες/σαχλαμάρες! *ti anoisíes/sachlamáres!*
I don't like... _____	Δε μου αρέσει... *dhe moo arési...*
I'm bored to death _____	Πλήττω φοβερά... *plíto foverá*
I've had enough_____	Βαρέθηκα πια *varéthika pya*
I can't take any more _____ of this	Δεν το ανέχομαι άλλο *dhen to anéchome álo*
I was expecting _____ something completely different	Περίμενα κάτι τελείως διαφορετικό *perímena káti telíos dhyaforetikó*

2

Courtesies

Conversation

Conversation

.1 **I** beg your pardon?

I don't speak any/ _____	Δε μιλάω/μιλάω λιγα...
I speak a little...	*dhe miláo/miláo lígha...*
I'm American _____	Είμαι Αμερικανικος
	íme amerikánikos
Do you speak _____	Μιλάτε αγγλικά/γαλλικά/γερμανικά;
English/French/German?	*miláte angliká/ghaliká/yermaniká?*
Is there anyone who_____	Ξέρει κανείς εδώ... ;
speaks...?	*xéri kanís edhó...?*
I beg your pardon? _____	Ορίστε;/Τι είπατε;
	oríste?/ti ípate?
I (don't) understand _____	(Δεν) καταλαβαίνω
	(dhen) katalavéno
Do you understand me? ___	Με καταλαβαίνετε;
	me katalavénete?
Could you repeat that, _____	Μπορείτε να το επαναλάβετε, παρακαλώ;
please?	*boríte na to epanalávete, parakaló;*
Could you speak more_____	Μπορείτε να μιλάτε πιο αργά, παρακαλώ;
slowly, please?	*boríte na miláte pyo arghá, parakaló?*
What does that (word)_____	Τι θα πει αυτό/αυτή η λέξη;
mean?	*ti tha pi aftó/aftí i léxi?*
Is that similar to/the _____	Είναι (περίπου) το ίδιο με... ;
same as...?	*íne (perípoo) to ídhyo me...?*
Could you write that_____	Μου το γράφετε, παρακαλώ;
down for me, please?	*moo to ghráfete, parakaló?*
Could you spell that _____	Μου το συλλαβίζετε, παρακαλώ;
for me, please?	*moo to silavízete, parakaló?*

(See 1.8 Telephone alphabet)

Could you point that_____	Μπορείτε να το δείξετε σ' αυτό τον οδηγό;
out in this phrase book,	*boríte na to dhíxete saftó tonodhighó?*
please?	
One moment, please,_____	Ένα λεπτό, πρέπει να το ψάξω πρώτα
I have to look it up	*éna leptó, prépi na to psáxo próta*
I can't find the word/the ___	Δεν μπορώ να βρω τη λέξη/τη φράση
sentence	*dhemboró na vro ti léxi/ti frási*
How do you say_____	Πώς λέγεται αυτό στα... ;
that in...?	*pos léyete aftó sta...?*
How do you pronounce_____	Πώς προφέρεται αυτό;
that?	*pos proférete aftó?*

Conversation

3.2 Introductions

May I introduce myself?	Επιτρέψτε μου να συστηθώ *epitrépste moo na sistithó*
My name's...	Λέγομαι.../Με λένε... *léghome.../me léne...*
I'm...	Είμαι...ο/η *íme...o/i*
What's your name?	Πώς λέγεσθε; / Πώς σας λένε; *pos léyesthe?/ pos sas léne?*
May I introduce...?	Επιτρέψτε μου να σας συστήσω *epitrépste moo na sas sistíso*
This is my wife/ daughter/mother/ girlfriend	Αυτή είναι η γυναίκα μου/η κόρη μου/η μητέρα μου/η φίλη μου *aftí íne i yinéka moo/i kóri moo/i mitéra moo/i fíli moo*
– my husband/son/ father/boyfriend	Αυτός είναι ο άντρας μου/ο γιός μου/ο πατέρας μου/ο φίλος μου *aftós íne o ándras moo/ o yos moo/o patéras moo/o fílos moo*
How do you do	Γειά σας, χαίρομαι για τη γνωριμία σας *ya sas, hérome ya ti ghnorimía sas*
Pleased to meet you	Χαίρω πολύ *héro polí*
Where are you from?	Από πού είστε; *apó poo íste?*
I'm from the United States	Είμαι απ' της Ηνωμενες Πολιτειες *íme apó tis enoménes poletíes*
What city do you live in?	Σε ποιά πόλη μένετε; *se pya póli ménete?*
In..., it's near...	Σε...Είναι κοντά σε... *se...íne kondá se*
Have you been here long?	Είστε πολύ καιρό εδώ; *íste polí keró edhó?*
A few days	Μερικές μέρες *merikés méres*
How long are you staying here?	Πόσο καιρό θα μείνετε εδώ; *póso kyeró tha mínete edhó?*
We're (probably) leaving tomorrow/in two weeks	(Μάλλον) θα φύγουμε αύριο/σε δύο εβδομάδες *(málon) tha fíghoome ávrio/se dhío evdhomádhes*
Where are you staying?	Που μένετε; *poo ménete?*
In a hotel/an apartment	Σ' ένα ξενοδοχείο/σε διαμέρισμα *séna xenodhohío/se dhiamérizma*
On a camp site	Σ' ένα κάμπινγκ *séna kámping*
With friends/relatives	Σε φίλους/σε συγγενείς *se fíloos/se singenís*
Are you here on your own/with your family?	Είστε μόνος σας /μόνη σας /με την οικόγενειά σας; *íste mónos sas/móni sas/me tin ikoyényásas?*

Conversation
3

I'm on my own	Είμαι μόνος μου /μόνη μου
	íme mónos moo/móni moo
I'm with my partner/wife/husband	Είμαι με το /τη σύντροφό μου/τη γυναίκα μου/τον άντρα μου
	íme me to/ti síndrofómoo/ti yinéka moo/ton ándra moo
– with my family	Είμαι με την οικογένειά μου
	íme me tin ikoyényámoo
– with relatives	Είμαι με συγγενείς μου
	íme me singenís moo
– with a friend/friends	Είμαι μ' ένα φίλο/με μία φίλη/με φίλους
	íme ména filo/me mya fíli/me fíloos
Are you married?	Είστε παντρεμένος/παντρεμένη;
	íste pandreménos/pandreméni?
Do you have a steady boyfriend/girlfriend?	Έχεις ένα φίλο/μια φιλενάδα;
	éhis éna fílo/mya filenádha?
That's none of your business	Δε σας ενδιαφέρει/Δε σας πέφτει λόγος
	dhe sas endhiaféri/dhe sas péfti lóghos
I'm married	Είμαι παντρεμένος/παντρεμένη
	íme pandreménos/pandreméni
– single	Είμαι εργένης
	íme eryénis
– separated	Είμαι χωρισμένος/χωρισμένη (από κλίνη και στέγη)
	íme chorizménos/chorizméni (apó klíni ke stéyi)
– divorced	Είμαι διεζευγμένος/διεζευγμένη
	íme dhiezevghménos/dhiezevghméni
– a widow/widower	Είμαι χήρα/χήρος
	íme híra/híros
I live alone/with someone	Μένω μόνος μου/μόνη μου/μαζί με το φίλο μου/τη φιλενάδα μου
	méno mónos moo/móni moo/mazí me to fílo moo/ti filenádha moo
Do you have any children/grandchildren?	Έχετε παιδιά/εγγόνια;
	éhete pedhyá/engónya?
How old are you?	Πόσων χρονών είστε;
	póson chronón íste?
How old is she/he?	Πόσων χρονών είναι;
	póson chronón íne?
I'm...	Είμαι...χρονών
	íme...chronón
She's/he's...	Είναι...χρονών
	íne...chronón
What do you do for a living?	Τί δουλειά κάνετε;
	ti dhoolyá kánete?
I work in an office	Δουλεύω σ' ένα γραφείο
	dhoolévo séna ghrafío
I'm a student/ I'm at school	Σπουδάζω/πηγαίνω σχολείο
	spoodházo/piyéno scholío
I'm unemployed	Είμαι άνεργος/άνεργη
	íme ánerghos/áneryi
I'm retired	Είμαι συνταξιούχος/συνταξιούχα
	íme sintaxióochos/sintaxióocha
I'm on a disability pension	Είμαι ανίκανος/ανίκανη για εργασία, έχω επίδομα ανικανότητας
	íme aníkanos/aníkani ya erghasía, ého epídhoma anikanótitas

I'm a housewife _____	Είμαι νοικοκυρά *íme nikokirá*
Do you like your job? _____	Σας αρέσει η δουλειά σας; *sas arési i dhoolyásas?*
Most of the time _____	Μερικές φορές ναι, μερικές φορές όχι *merikés forés ne, merikés forés óhi*
I usually do, but I prefer ___ vacations	Συνήθως μ' αρέσει, αλλά οι διακοπές μ' αρέσουν πιο πολύ *siníthos marési, alá i dhiakopés marésoon pyo polí*

3.3 Starting/ending a conversation

Could I ask you _____ something?	Μπορώ να σας ρωτήσω κάτι; *boró na sas rotíso káti?*
Excuse me_____	Με συγχωρείτε *me sinchoríte*
Excuse me, could you _____ help me?	Συγγνώμη, μήπως μπορείτε να με βοηθήσετε; *signómi, mípos boríte na me voithísete?*
Yes, what's the problem? __	Ναι, ποιό είναι το πρόβλημά σας; *ne, pyo íne to próvlimásas?*
What can I do for you? ____	Τί μπορώ να κάνω για σας; *ti boró na káno ya sas?*
Sorry, I don't have time ____ now	Λυπάμαι, δεν έχω καιρό τώρα *lipáme, dhen écho keró tóra*
Do you have a light? _____	Μήπως έχετε φωτιά; *mípos éhete fotyá?*
May I join you? _____	Μπορώ να καθίσω δίπλα σας; *boró na kathíso dhípla sas?*
Could you take a _____ picture of me/us? Press this button	Μπορείτε να με/μας βγάλετε μια φωτογραφία; Να πιέστε αυτό το κουμπί *boríte na me/mas vghálete mya fotografía? na pyéste avtó to koobí*
Leave me alone _____	Ασε με ήσυχο *áse me ísicho*
Get lost_____	Εξαφανίσου *exafanísoo*
Go away or I'll scream_____	Αν δε φύγετε, θα βάλω τις φωνές *an dhe fíyete, tha válo tis fonés*

3.4 Congratulations and condolences

Happy birthday/many_____ happy returns	Χρόνια πολλά *chrónya polá*
Please accept my_____ condolences	Τα συλλυπητήριά μου *ta silipitíryámoo*
I'm very sorry for you _____	Ηταν μεγάλο πλήγμα *ítan meghálo plíghma*

3.5 A chat about the weather

See also 1.5 The weather

It's so hot/cold today!_____	Τί ζέστη/κρύο που κάνει σήμερα! *ti zésti/krío poo káni símera!*
Nice weather, isn't it?_____	Τί ωραίος καιρός, ε; *ti oréos kerós, e?*

What a wind/storm! _____	Τί αέρας/θύελλα!
	ti aéras/thíela!
All that rain/snow! _____	Τί βροχή/χιόνι!
	ti vrohí/hyóni!
All that fog! _____	Τί ομίχλη!
	ti omíchli!
How long has the _____ weather been like this here?	Από πότε κάνει τέτοιον καιρό εδώ; apó póte káni tétyo keró edhó?
Is it always this hot/cold ___ here?	Πάντα κάνει τόση ζέστη/τόσο κρύο εδώ; pánda káni tósi zésti/tóso krío edhó?
Is it always this dry/wet____ here?	Έχει πάντα εδώ τόση ξηρασία/υγρασία; éhi pánda edhó tósi xirasía/ighrasía?

 .6 Hobbies

Do you have any _____ hobbies?	Έχετε χόμπυ; éhete hóbi?
I like painting/_____ reading/photography	Μ' αρέσει να πλέκω/να διαβάζω/η φωτογραφία marési na pléko/na dhiavázo/i fotoghrafía
I like music _____	Αγαπώ τη μουσική aghapó ti moosikí
I like playing the _____ guitar/piano	Μ' αρέσει να παίζω κιθάρα/πιάνο marési na pézo kithára/pyáno
I like going to the _____ movies	Μ' αρέσει να πηγαίνω στον κινηματογράφο marési na piyéno stonginimatoghráfo
I like travelling/playing_____ sports/fishing/walking	Μ' αρέσει να ταξιδεύω/να κάνω σπορ/να ψαρεύω/να πηγαίνω περίπατο marési na taxidhévo/na káno spor/na psarévo/na piyéno perípato

 .7 Being the host(ess)

See also 4 Eating out

Can I offer you a drink? ____	Μπορώ να σας προσφέρω ένα ποτό; boró na sas prosféro éna potó?
What would you like_____ to drink?	Τί θέλεις να πιεις; ti thélis na pyis?
Would you like a _____ cigarette/cigar?	Θέλετε ένα τσιγάρο/ένα πούρο; thélete éna tsigháro/éna póoro?
Something non-_____ alcoholic, please	Θα ήθελα ένα ποτό χωρίς αλκοόλ/ένα αναψυκτικό tha íthela éna potó chorís alkól/éna anapsiktikó
I don't smoke _____	Δεν καπνίζω dhen kapnízo

 .8 Invitations

| Are you doing anything____ tonight? | Είσαι ελεύθερος/ελεύθερη απόψε; íse eléftheros/eléftheri apópse? |
| Do you have any plans ____ for today/this afternoon/tonight? | Έχετε κανένα πρόγραμμα για σήμερα/για το απόγευμα/για απόψε; éhete kanéna próghrama ya símera/ya to apóyevma/ya apópse? |

Would you like to go out with me?	Θα θέλατε να βγούμε έξω μαζί; *tha thélate na vghóome éxo mazí?*
Would you like to go dancing with me?	Θα θέλατε να πάμε να χορέψουμε μαζί; *tha thélate na páme na chorépsoome mazí?*
Would you like to have lunch/dinner with me?	Θα θέλατε να πάμε να φάμε μαζί; *tha thélate na páme na fáme mazí?*
Would you like to come to the beach with me?	Θα θέλατε να πάμε μαζί στην παραλία; *tha thélate na páme mazí stimbaralía?*
Would you like to come into town with us?	Θα θέλατε να' ρθείτε μαζί μας στην πόλη; *tha thélate narthíte mazí mas stimbóli?*
Would you like to come and see some friends with us?	Θα θέλατε να' ρθείτε μαζί μας σε φίλους μας; *tha thélate narthíte mazí mas se fíloos mas?*
Shall we dance?	Πάμε να χορέψουμε; *páme na chorépsoome?*
– sit at the bar?	Πάμε να καθίσουμε στο μπαρ; *páme na kathísoome sto bar?*
– get something to drink?	Πάμε να πιούμε κάτι; *páme na pyóome káti?*
– go for a walk/drive?	Πάμε να κάνουμε μια βόλτα/μια βόλτα με το αυτοκίνητο; *páme na kánoome mya vólta/mya vólta me to aftokínito*
Yes, all right	Ναι, εντάξει *ne, endáxi*
Good idea	Καλή ιδέα *kalí idhéa*
No (thank you)	Οχι, (ευχαριστώ) *óhi (efcharistó)*
Maybe later	Ισως αργότερα *ísos arghótera*
I don't feel like it	Δεν έχω όρεξη *dhen écho órexi*
I don't have time	Δεν έχω καιρό *dhen écho keró*
I already have a date	Εχω ένα άλλο ραντεβού *écho éna álo randevóo*
I'm not very good at dancing/volleyball/ swimming	Δεν ξέρω να χορεύω/να παίζω βόλλευ/να κολυμπώ *dhen xéro na chorévo/na pézo vóllei/na kolimbó*

3 .9 Paying a compliment

You look wonderful!	Είστε μια χαρά! *íste mya chará!*
I like your car!	Τί ωραίο αυτοκίνητο! *ti oréo aftokínito!*
You're a nice boy/girl	Είσαι πολύ καλό παιδί/κορίτσι *íse polí kaló pedhí/korítsi*
What a sweet child!	Τί γλυκό παιδάκι! *ti ghlikó pedháki!*
You're a wonderful dancer!	Χορεύετε πολύ καλά *chorévete polí kalá*
You're a wonderful cook!	Μαγειρεύετε πολύ καλά *mayirévete polí kalá*
You're a terrific soccer player!	Παίζετε πολύ καλά ποδόσφαιρο *pézete polí kalá podhósfero*

.10 Intimate comments/questions

I like being with you	Μ' αρέσει να είμαι μαζί σου
	marési na íme mazí soo
I've missed you so much	Μου έλειψες πολύ
	moo élipses polí
I dreamt about you	Σε είδα στ' όνειρό μου
	se ídha stoniró moo
I think about you all day	Δε βγαίνεις από το νου μου
	dhe vyénis apó to noo moo
You have such a sweet smile	Έχεις ένα γλυκό χαμόγελο
	éhis éna ghlikó chamóyelo
You have such beautiful eyes	Έχεις πολύ ωραία μάτια
	éhis polí oréa mátya
I'm in love with you	Είμαι ερωτευμένος/ερωτευμένη μαζί σου
	íme erotevménos/erotevméni mazí soo
I'm in love with you too	Κι εγώ με σένα
	kyeghó me séna
I love you	Σ' αγαπώ
	saghapó
I love you too	Κι εγώ σ' αγαπώ
	kyeghó saghapó
I don't feel as strongly about you	Εγώ δεν έχω τέτοια σοβαρά αισθήματα για σένα
	eghó dhen écho tétya sovará esthímata ya séna
I already have a boyfriend/girlfriend	Έχω ήδη φίλο/φιλενάδα
	écho idhi fílo/filenádha
I'm not ready for that	Δεν είμαι έτοιμος/έτοιμη γι' αυτό
	dhen íme étimos/étimi yaftó
This is going too fast for me	Καλύτερα να μη βιαζόμαστε τόσο
	kalítera na mi viazómaste tóso
Take your hands off me	Μη μ' αγγίζεις
	mi mangízis
Okay, no problem	Εντάξει, δεν πειράζει
	endáxi, dhembirázi
Will you stay with me tonight?	Θα μείνεις μαζί μου τη νύχτα;
	tha mínis mazí moo ti níchta
I'd like to go to bed with you	Θέλω να κάνουμε έρωτα
	thélo na kánoome érota
Only if we use a condom	Μόνο με προφυλακτικό
	móno me profilaktikó
We have to be careful about AIDS	Πρέπει να προσέχουμε λόγω του ΕΙΤΖ
	prépi na proséchoome lógho too AIDS
That's what they all say	Όλοι τα ίδια λένε
	óli ta ídhya léne
We shouldn't take any risks	Ας μη το διακινδυνέψουμε
	mi to dhiakindhinépsoome
Do you have a condom?	Έχεις προφυλακτικό;
	éhis profilaktikó?
No? In that case we won't do it	Όχι; Τότε δε γίνεται
	óhi? tóte dhe yínete

Conversation

3.11 Arrangements

When will I see you again?	Πότε θα σε ξαναδώ; *póte tha se xanadhó?*
Are you free over the weekend?	Θα έχετε καιρό το Σαββατοκύριακο; *tha éhete keró to savatokíriako?*
What shall we do?	Τί θα κανονίσουμε; *ti tha kanonísoome?*
Where shall we meet?	Πού θα συναντηθούμε; *poo tha sinandithóome?*
Will you pick me/us up?	Θα 'ρθείτε να με/μας πάρετε; *tharthíte na me/mas párete?*
Shall I pick you up?	Να περάσω να σας πάρω; *na peráso na sas páro?*
I have to be home by...	Πρέπει να είμαι σπίτι στις... *prépi na íme spíti stis...*
Can I take you home?	Μπορώ να σας πάω σπίτι; *boró na sas páo spíti?*
I don't want to see you anymore	Δε θέλω να σας ξαναδώ *dhe thélo na sas xanadhó*

3.12 Saying good-bye

Can I write/call you?	Μπορώ να σας γράψω/τηλεφωνήσω; *boró na sas ghrápso/tilefoníso?*
Will you write/call me?	Θα μου γράψετε/τηλεφωνήσετε; *tha moo ghrápsete/tilefonísete?*
Can I have your address/phone number?	Μπορώ να έχω τη διεύθυνση σας/τον αριθμό του τηλεφώνου σας; *boró na écho ti dhiésthinsi sas/ton arithmó too tilefónoo sas?*
Thanks for everything	Ευχαριστώ για όλα *efcharistó ya óla*
It was very nice	Ήταν πολύ ωραία *ítan polí oréa*
Say hello to...	Χαιρετισμούς σε *heretizmóos se...*
All the best	Σου εύχομαι ό,τι καλύτερο *soo éfchome óti kalítero*
Good luck	Καλή επιτυχία στο μέλλον *kalí epitihía sto mélon*
When will you be back?	Πότε θα ξαναέρθεις; *póte tha xanaérthis?*
I'll be waiting for you	Θα σε περιμένω *tha se periméno*
I'd like to see you again	Θα ήθελα πολύ να σε ξαναδώ *tha íthela polí na se xanadhó*
I hope we meet again soon	Ελπίζω να ξαναιδωθούμε σύντομα *elpízo na xanaidhothóome síndoma*
This is our address. If you're ever in the US...	Αυτή είναι η διεύθυνσή μας. Αν κάποτε βρεθείτε στης Ηνωμένες Πολιτειες... *aftí íne i dhiéfthinsí mas. an kápote vrethíte stis enoménes poletíes...*
You'd be more than welcome	Είστε πάντα ευπρόσδεκτος/ευπρόσδεκτη *íste pánda efprósdhektos/efprósdhekti*

Eating out

● **In Greece** people usually have three meals:
1 *το πρωινό* (breakfast), between 7.00 and 10.00am. Breakfast is light and consists of a cup of coffee with bread and jam or honey.
2 *το γεύμα* (lunch), between 1.00 and 3.00pm. Lunch always includes a hot dish and is the most important meal of the day.
3 *το δείπνο* (dinner), between 9.00pm and 1.00am. Dinner is a hot meal similar to lunch though a little lighter. It is usually taken with the family.

 .1 On arrival

I'd like to reserve a table for seven o'clock, please	Μπορώ να κλείσω ένα τραπέζι γι' απόψε στις εφτά;
	boró na klíso éna trapézi yapópse stis eftá?
I'd like a table for two, please	Θα ήθελα ένα τραπέζι για δύο άτομα
	tha íthela éna trapézi ya dhío átoma
We've/we haven't reserved	(Δεν) κλείσαμε τραπέζι
	(dhen) klísame trapézi
Is the restaurant open yet?	Είναι ανοιχτή η κουζίνα;
	íne anichtí i koozína?
What time does the restaurant open/close?	Πότε ανοίγει/κλείνει η κουζίνα;
	póte aníyi/klíni i koozína?
Can we wait for a table?	Μπορούμε να περιμένουμε για ένα τραπέζι;
	boróome na periménoome ya éna trapézi?
Will we have to wait long?	Θα πρέπει να περιμένουμε πολλή ώρα;
	tha prépi na periménoome polí óra?
Is this seat taken?	Είναι ελεύθερη αυτή η θέση;
	íne eléftheri aftí i thési?
Could we sit here/there?	Μπορούμε να καθίσουμε εδώ/εκεί;
	boróome na kathísoome edhó/ekí?
Can we sit by the window?	Μπορούμε να καθίσουμε κοντά στο παράθυρο;
	boróome na kathísoome kondá sto paráthiro?
Can we eat outside?	Μπορούμε να φάμε κι έξω;
	boróome na fáme kyéxo?
Do you have another chair for us?	Μας φέρνετε ακόμα μια καρέκλα;
	mas férnete akóma mya karékla?
Do you have a highchair?	Μας φέρνετε μια παιδική καρέκλα;
	mas férnete mya pedhikí karékla?
Is there an outlet (a socket) this bottle-warmer?	Υπάρχει μια πρίζα γι' αυτό το βραστήρα;
	ipárhi mya príza yavtó to vrastíra?

Κλείσατε τραπέζι;	Do you have a reservation?
Με ποιό όνομα;	What name, please?
Από δω, παρακαλώ	This way, please
Αυτό το τραπέζι είναι κλεισμένο	This table is reserved
Σ' ένα τέταρτο θα 'χουμε ελεύθερο τραπέζι	We'll have a table free in fifteen minutes
Μπορείτε να περιμένετε στο (μπαρ);	Would you like to wait (at the bar)?

Could you warm up _____ this bottle/jar for me?	Μπορείτε να μου ζεστάνετε αυτό το μπιμπερό/βαζάκι;
	boríte na moo zestánete avtó to biberó/vazáki?
Not too hot, please _____	Να μην είναι πολύ ζεστό, παρακαλώ
	na min íne polí zestó, parakaló
Is there somewhere I _____ can change the baby's diaper?	Υπάρχει κάποιος χώρος όπου μπορώ να αλλάξω το μωρό;
	ipárhi kápyos chóros ópoo boró na aláxo to moró?
Where are the restrooms? _	Πού είναι η τουαλέτα;
	poo íne i twaléta?

4 .2 Ordering

Waiter!/Madam!/Sir!_____	Γκαρσόνι!/Κυρία/Κύριε!
	garsóni!/kiría!/kírie!
We'd like something to ___ eat/a drink	Θέλουμε να φάμε/να πιούμε κάτι
	théloome na fáme/na pyóome káti
Could I have a quick_____ meal?	Μπορώ να φάω κάτι γρήγορα;
	boró na fáo káti ghríghora?
We don't have much _____ time	Βιαζόμαστε
	viazómaste
We'd like to have a _____ drink first	Θέλουμε πρώτα να πιούμε κάτι
	théloome próta na pyóome káti
Could we see the_____ menu/wine list, please?	Μπορούμε να δούμε τον κατάλογο/τον κατάλογο κρασιών;
	boróome na dhóome tongatálogho/tongatálogho krasyón?
Do you have a menu _____ in English?	Έχετε ένα κατάλογο στα αγγλικά;
	éhete éna katálogho sta angliká?
Do you have a dish_____ of the day?/Do you have a tourist menu?	Έχετε πιάτο της ημέρας/τουριστικό μενού;
	éhete pyáto tis iméras/tooristikó menóo?
We haven't made a _____ choice yet	Δεν αποφασίσαμε ακόμα
	dhen apofasísame akóma
What do you _____ recommend?	Τί μπορείτε να μας προτείνετε;
	ti boríte na mas protínete?
What are the specialities ___ of the region/the house?	Ποιές είναι οι σπεσιαλιτέ της περιοχής/του μαγαζιού;
	pyes íne i spesialité tis periohís/too maghazyóo?
I like strawberries/olives ___	Μ' αρέσουν οι φράουλες/οι ελιές
	marésoon i fráooles/i elyés
I don't like fish/meat... _____	Δε μ' αρέσει το ψάρι/το κρέας/...
	dhe marési to psári/to kréas/...
What's this?_____	Τί είναι αυτό;
	ti íne aftó?
Does it have...in it? _____	Έχει μέσα...;
	éhi mésa...?
What does it taste like? ___	Με τί μοιάζει;
	me ti myázi?
Is this a hot or a_____ cold dish?	Αυτό το φαγητό είναι κρύο ή ζεστό;
	aftó to fayitó íne krío i zestó?
Is this sweet? _____	Αυτό το φαγητό είναι γλυκό;
	aftó to fayitó íne ghlikó?

Is this spicy/hot? _____	Αυτό το φαγητό είναι πικάντικο/πιπεράτο; *aftó to fayitó íne pikándiko/piperáto?*
Do you have _____ anything else?	Μήπως έχετε κάτι άλλο; *mípos éhete káti álo?*
I'm on a salt-free diet _____	Απαγορεύεται να τρώω αλάτι *apaghorévete na tró-o aláti*
I can't eat pork _____	Απαγορεύεται να τρώω χοιρινό κρέας *apaghorévete na tró-o hirinó kréas*
– sugar _____	Απαγορεύεται να τρώω ζάχαρη *apaghorévete na tró-o záchari*
– fatty foods _____	Απαγορεύεται να τρώω λίπη *apaghorévete na tró-o lípi*
– (hot) spices _____	Απαγορεύεται να τρώω (καυτερά) μπαχαρικά *apaghorévete na tró-o (kafterá) bachariká*
I'll/we'll have what those___ people are having	Θέλουμε το ίδιο φαγητό που τρώνε εκείνοι οι άνθρωποι, παρακαλώ *théloome to ídhyo fayitó poo tróne ekíni i ánthropi, parakaló*
I'd like... _____	Θα ήθελα... *tha íthela ...*
We're not having a _____ starter	Δε θέλουμε ορεκτικό *dhe théloome orektikó*
The child will share what __ we're having	Το παιδί θα φάει λίγο από το δικό μας φαγητό *to pedhí tha fái lígho apó to dhikó mas fayitó*
Could I have some _____ more bread, please?	Παρακαλώ, λίγο ψωμί ακόμα *parakaló, lígho psomí akóma*
– a bottle of water/wine____	Παρακαλώ, ένα μπουκάλι νερό/κρασί ακόμα *parakaló, éna bookáli neró/krasí akóma*
– another helping of... _____	Παρακαλώ, μια μερίδα... ακόμα *parakaló, mya merídha ... akóma*
– some salt and pepper ____	Μας φέρνετε το αλατοπίπερο, παρακαλώ; *mas férnete to alatopípero, parakaló?*
– a napkin _____	Μας φέρνετε μια χαρτοπετσέτα, παρακαλώ; *mas férnete mya chartopetséta, parakaló*
– a spoon _____	Μας φέρνετε ένα κουταλάκι, παρακαλώ; *mas férnete éna kootaláki, parakaló?*
– an ashtray _____	Μας φέρνετε ένα τασάκι, παρακαλώ; *mas férnete éna tasáki, parakaló?*
– some matches_____	Μας φέρνετε σπίρτα, παρακαλώ; *mas férnete spírta, parakaló?*
– some toothpicks_____	Μας φέρνετε οδοντογλυφίδες, παρακαλώ; *mas férnete odhondoghlifídhes, parakaló?*
– a glass of water _____	Μας φέρνετε ένα ποτήρι νερό, παρακαλώ; *mas férnete éna potíri neró, parakaló?*
– a straw (for the child) ____	Μας φέρνετε ένα καλαμάκι (για το παιδί), παρακαλώ; *mas férnete éna kalamáki (ya to pédhi), parakaló?*
Enjoy your meal!_____	Καλή όρεξη! *kalí órexi!*

Θέλετε να φάτε; _____	Do you want to eat?
Διαλέξατε τί θέλετε να φάτε;_____	Have you decided what you want?
Θέλετε ένα απεριτίφ; _____	Would you like a drink first?
Τί θέλετε να πιείτε;_____	What would you like to drink?
Καλή όρεξη _____	Enjoy your meal
Θέλετε ένα γλυκό/ένα καφέ; _____	Would you like a dessert/coffee?

You too! _____	Επίσης
	epísis
Cheers! _____	Στην υγειά σας!
	stin iyá sas!
The next round's on me ___	Το επόμενο κέρασμα είναι δικό μου
	to epómeno kyérazma íne dhikó moo
Could we have a doggy_____ bag, please?	Μπορούμε να πάρουμε τ' απομεινάρια για το σκύλο μας;
	boróome na pároome tapominária ya to skílo mas?

4.3 The bill

See also 8.2 Settling the bill

How much is this dish? ____	Πόσο κάνει αυτό το φαγητό;
	póso káni aftó to fayitó?
Could I have the bill, _____ please?	Το λογαριασμό, παρακαλώ
	to loghariazmó, parakaló
All together _____	Ολα μαζί
	óla mazí
Everyone pays separately__	Ο καθένας πληρώνει τα δικά του
	o kathénas plróni ta dhiká too
Could we have the menu __ again, please?	Μπορούμε να ξαναδούμε τον κατάλογο;
	boróome na xanadhóome tongatálogho?
The...is not on the bill _____	Το...δεν είναι στο λογαριασμό
	to...dhen íne sto loghariazmó

4.4 Complaints

It's taking a very_____ long time	Αργείτε πολύ
	aryíte polí
We've been here an _____ hour already	Περιμένουμε ήδη μια ώρα
	periménoome ídhi mya óra
This must be a mistake ____	Πρέπει να έγινε κάποιο λάθος
	prépi na éyine kápyo láthos
This is not what I_____ ordered	Δεν παράγγειλα αυτό
	dhen parángila avtó
I ordered... _____	Παράγγειλα...
	parángila...
There's a dish missing_____	Λείπει ένα φαγητό
	lípi éna fayitó

This is broken/not clean ___	Αυτό είναι σπασμένο/δεν είναι καθαρό
	aftó íne spazméno/dhen íne katharó
The food's cold _____	Το φαγητό είναι κρύο
	to fayitó íne krío
– not fresh _____	Το φαγητό δεν είναι φρέσκο
	to fayitó dhen íne frésko
– too salty/sweet/spicy____	Το φαγητό είναι πολύ αλμυρό/γλυκό/πικάντικο
	to fayitó íne polí almiró/ghlikó/pikándiko
The meat's not done_____	Το κρέας δεν είναι ψημένο
	to kréas dhen íne psiméno
– overdone _____	Το κρέας είναι πολύ ψημένο
	to kréas íne polí psiméno
– tough _____	Το κρέας είναι σκληρό
	to kréas íne sklró
– spoiled_____	Το κρέας είναι χαλασμένο
	to kréas íne chalazméno
Could I have something ___ else instead of this?	Μπορείτε να μου δώσετε κάτι άλλο;
	boríte na moo dhósete káti álo?
The bill/this amount is _____ not right	Ο λογαριασμός/αυτό το ποσό δεν είναι σωστός/σωστό
	o loghariazmós/aftó to posó dhen íne sostós/sostó
We didn't have this _____	Αυτό δεν το είχαμε
	aftó dhen to íchame
There's no toilet paper_____ in the bathroom	Δεν έχει χαρτί στην τουαλέτα
	dhen éhi chartí stin twaléta
Do you have a _____ complaints book?	Εχετε βιβλίο παραπόνων;
	éhete vivlío parapónon?
Will you call the_____ manager, please?	Φωνάξτε το αφεντικό σας, παρακαλώ
	fonáxte to afendikósas, parakaló

🍴 .5 Paying a compliment

That was a wonderful _____ meal	Φάγαμε πολύ καλά
	fághame polí kalá
The food was excellent ____	Ηταν πολύ νόστιμο
	ítan polí nóstimo
The...in particular was _____ delicious	Προπαντός το...ήταν εξαιρετικό
	propandós to...ítan exeretikó

αλκοολούχα ποτά	λαχανικά	σούπες
alcoholic beverages	vegetables	soups
απεριτίφ	μεζέδες	σπεσιαλιτέ
aperitif	mixed starters (also	speciality
επιδόρπια	used when drinking	συμπεριλαμβανομένης
dessert	ouzo)	υπηρεσίας
ζεστά φαγητά	ντόπια φαγητά	tip included
hot dishes	local dishes	της σχάρας
θαλασσινά	ορεκτικά	grilled dishes
seafood	appetizers	της ώρας
κατά προτίμηση	πάστες	prepared while you wait
prepared as you want it	cakes/pastries	Φ.Π.Α.
κατάλογος κρασιών	πιάτα της ημέρας	VAT
wine list	dish of the day	φαγητά για
κρέας	πουλερικά	χορτοφάγους
meat	poultry	vegetarian dishes
κρύα φαγητά	πρωινό	ψάρι
cold dishes	breakfast	fish

αγγούρι	βερύκοκα	γίγαντες
cucumber	apricots	large white beans
αγκινάρες	βοδινό κρέας	γιουβαρλάκια
globe artichokes	beef	meatballs
αλάτι	βούτυρο	γιουβέτσι
salt	butter	a form of pasta
αμύγδαλο (-λα)	βραστό	γλώσσα
almond(s)	boiled	sole (fish)
αντίδια	βυσσινάδα	γραβιέρα
endives	sour cherry	cheese
αντσούγιες	drink	γρανίτα
anchovies	γάλα	a drink made
αρακάς	milk	with crushed ice
peas	γαλακτομπούρεκο	and fruit
αρνί/αρνίσιο κρέα	cake made with	δαμάσκηνο (-να)
lamb	filo pastry	plums/prunes
αστακός	and confectioner's	δάφνη
lobster	custard	bayleaf
αυγά μάτι	γαλλόπουλο	ελιές
fried eggs	turkey	olives
αυγολέμονο	γαρίδες	ζαμπόν
egg and lemon	prawns	ham
(sauce or soup)	γεμιστό	ζάχαρη
αχλάδι(α)	stuffed	sugar
pear(s)	γιαούρτι	ζουμί
βασιλόπιτα	yogurt	broth
New Year's cake	γιαχνί	θυμάρι
βατόμουρα	a stew	thyme
blackberries		

Eating out

ιμάμ-μπαϊλτί
a dish of eggplants
  baked with tomato
  and garlic
καβούρι
crab
κακαβιά
a fish soup
καλαμαράκι
squid
καλαμπόκι
corn on the cob
καραβίδα
crayfish
καραμέλλα
a boiled dessert
καρότα
carrots
καρπούζι
water melon
καρύδια
walnuts
κασέρι
hard parmesan-like
  cheese
κάστανο
chestnut
καταΐφι
a cake made
  with honey, and
  nuts
κατσικάκι
kid
καφές
coffee
καφές φραπέ
iced coffee
κεράσι (α)
cherry (cherries)
κεφαλοτύρι
hard cheese
κεφτέδες
fried meatballs
κιμάς
ground meat
κίτρο
lime
κοκκινιστό
baked in a tomato
  sauce
κοκορέτσι
tripe cooked on a
  skewer
κολοκυθάκι
zucchini

κολοκύθι
marrow/pumpkin
κομπόστα
compote
κοτόπουλο
chicken
κουκιά
broad beans
κουλουράκι (α)
small ring-shaped
  crackers
κουλούρι
hard ring-shaped
  sesame bread
κουνέλι
rabbit
κουραμπιέδες
cakes made with
  almonds and caster
  sugar
κρασί
wine
κρέας
meat
κρέμα
confectioner's custard
κρεμμύδι(α)
onion(s)
κυνήγι
game
λαγός
hare
λάδι
oil
λαχανάκια
  Βρυξελλών
Brussels sprouts
λαχανικό (-κά)
vegetable(s)
λάχανο
cabbage
λεμονάδα
lemonade
λεμόνι
lemon
λουκάνικα
sausages
λουκουμάδες
light doughnuts served
  with spiced honey
λουκούμι
Turkish Delight
μαγειρίτσα
an Easter soup made
  from lamb and
  goat entrails

μαϊντανό
parsley
μανιτάρι
mushrooms
μανούρι
a white cheese
μαρίδες
whitebait
μαρμελάδα
jam
μαρούλι
lettuce
μέλι
honey
μελιτζάνα
eggplant
μελομακάρονα
cakes made of honey
  and nuts
μήλο
apple
μιζήθρα
a soft goat's cheese
μοσχάρι/μοσχαρίσιο
  κρέας
veal
μοσχοκάρυδο
nutmeg
μούρο
mulberry
μουσακάς
a dish made with
  layers of chopped
  lamb and eggplant
μούσμουλα
loquat
μουστάρδα
mustard
μπακαλιάρος
dried cod
μπακλαβάς
cake made with filo
  pastry, nuts and
  honey
μπάμιες
okra
μπαρμπούνι
red mullet
μπιζέλια
peas
μπιφτέκι
burger

μπουγάτσα
a cake made with
filo pastry and
confectioner's
custard

μπούτι
thigh

μπριζόλα βοδινή
beef chop/cutlet

μπύρα
beer

μυαλά
brains

μύδια
mussels

νερό
water

νεφρά
kidneys

ντολμάδες
stuffed vine-leaves

ντομάτες
tomatoes

ντομάτες
  γεμιστές
stuffed tomatoes

ξηροί καρποί
dried fruit

ξίδι/ξύδι
vinegar

ομελέτα
omelette

ούζο
ouzo (aniseed-
flavored spirit)

ουίσκυ
whiskey

παγωτό
ice cream

παϊδάκι
lamb chop

παντζάρια
beet

πάπια
duck

παπουτσάκια
stuffed eggplants

πάστες
cakes

παστίτσιο
ground meat and
  macaroni pie

παστό
salted

πατάτες
potatoes

πατσάς
soup made from
  tripe

πεπόνι
melon

πέστροφα
trout

πετεινάρι κρασάτο
coq au vin

πιλάφι
pilaf rice

πιπέρι
pepper

πιπεριά
green or red pepper
  (vegetable)

πιτσούνι
young pigeons

πλάτη
shoulder

πορτοκαλάδα
orange juice/
  soda

πορτοκάλι
orange

πράσο
leek

ραδίκια
chicory

ραπανάκια
radishes

ρεβύθια
chick-peas

ρέγγα
herring (smoked)

ρετσίνα
wine flavored with
  pine resin

ρίγανη
oregano

ροδάκινο
peach

ρόδι
pomegranate

ρύζι
rice

ρυζόγαλο
rice pudding

σαλάτα
salad

σαλιγγάρια
snails

σάλτσα
sauce

σαντιγί
whipped cream

σάντουιτς
sandwich

σαρδέλλες
sardines

σέλινο
celery

σκορδαλιά
dip made from garlic
  and bread or
  potato

σκόρδο
garlic

σκουμπρί
mackerel

σοκολάτα
chocolate

σολομός
salmon

σουβλάκι
grilled meat on a
  skewer

σούπα
soup

σουπιές
cuttle fish

σουτζουκάκια
spicy meatballs in
  tomato sauce

σπανάκι
spinach

στα κάρβουνα
barbecued

σταφύλια
grapes

στη σχάρα
on the grill

στιφάδο
stew made with
  shallots and
  flavored with sweet
  wine

στο φούρνο
cooked in the oven

στρείδι
oysters

σύκα
figs

συκώτι
liver

σφυρίδα
grey mullet

ταραμάς
smoked cod's roe

ταραμοσαλάτα
paste made from
  smoked cod's roe

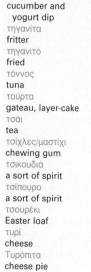

τασκεμπάμπ
shish kebab

τζατζίκι
cucumber and
   yogurt dip

τηγανίτα
fritter

τηγανιτό
fried

τόννος
tuna

τούρτα
gateau, layer-cake

τσάι
tea

τσίχλες/μαστίχι
chewing gum

τσικουδιά
a sort of spirit

τσίπουρο
a sort of spirit

τσουρέκι
Easter loaf

τυρί
cheese

Τυρόπιτα
cheese pie

φασκόμηλο
aromatic herb tea

φασολάκια
green beans

φασόλια
haricot beans

φέτα
goat's cheese

φιλέτο
fillet steak

φουντούκια
hazelnuts

φράουλες
strawberries

φράπα
a variety of grapefruit

φρούτο
fruit

φρυγανιά
toast, French-style

φυστίκια
pistachio nuts

χαβιάρι
caviar

χαλβάς
a dessert made with
   semolina, honey
   and nuts

χαμομήλι
chamomile

χέλι
eel

χήνα
goose

χοιρινό
pork

χόρτα
green dandelion
   leaves used in
   salad

χουρμάς
date

χταπόδι
octopus

χυμός
juice

χωριάτικη σαλάτα
a salad made
from tomatoes,
cucumber, black
olives and goat's
cheese

ψάρι
fish

ψητό
roast/baked

ψωμί
bread

5

On the road

5 .1 **A**sking for directions

Excuse me, could I ask you something? — Συγγνώμη, μπορώ να σας ρωτήσω κάτι;
sighnómi, boró na sas rotíso káti?

I've lost my way — Έχασα το δρόμο
échasa to dhrómo

Is there a(n)... around here? — Ξέρετε κανένα...εδώ κοντά;
xérete kanéna...edhó kondá?

Is this the way to...? — Αυτός είναι ο δρόμος για...;
aftós íne o dhrómos ya...?

Could you tell me how to get to... (name of place) — Μπορείτε να μου πείτε πώς μπορώ να πάω σε... ;
boríte na moo píte pos boró na páo se...?

What's the quickest way to...? — Ποιός είναι ο πιο σύντομος δρόμος για... ;
pyos íne o pyo síndomos dhrómos ya ...?

How many kilometers is it to...? — Πόσα χιλιόμετρα είναι ακόμα ως...;
pósa hilyómetra íne akóma os...?

Could you point it out on the map? — Μπορείτε να το δείξετε στο χάρτη;
boríte na to dhíxete sto chartí?

Δεν ξέρω, δεν είμαι από δω — I don't know, I don't know my way around here

Πήρατε λάθος δρόμο — You're going the wrong way

Πρέπει να γυρίσετε σε... — You have to go back to...

Εκεί θ' ακολουθήσετε τις πινακίδες — From there on just follow the signs

Εκεί θα ξαναρωτήσετε — When you get there, ask again

ίσια
straight ahead

αριστερά
left

δεξιά
right

στρίβω
turn

ακολουθώ
follow

περνάω το δρόμο
cross the road

η διασταύρωση
the intersection

ο δρόμος/η οδός
the street

το φανάρι
the traffic light

το τούνελ
the tunnel

η πινακίδα διασταύρωση προτεραιότητας
the `yield' sign

το κτίριο
the building

στη γωνιά
at the corner

το ποτάμι
the river

η ανισόπεδη διασταύρωση
the overpass

η γέφυρα
the bridge

η διάβαση του τρένου/οι μπάρες
the grade crossing

η πινακίδα που δείχνει το δρόμο για...
the sign pointing to...

το βέλος
the arrow

● **Border documents:** valid passport. For car and motorcycle: valid US driving license and registration document, insurance document, green card, US registration plate. Trailer: must be entered on the green card and driven with the same registration number. A warning cone, headlight converters and extra headlight bulbs should be carried. Insurance should also be upgraded.

Import and export specifications:

Foreign currency: a maximum of 100,000 drachmas may be taken into the country, and a maximum of 20,000 may be taken out.

Alcohol (aged 18 and above): 1 and a half liters of spirits, fortified or sparkling wine. Tobacco (aged 17 and above): 300 cigarettes or 150 cigars or 400 grams of tobacco.

Το διαβατήριό σας, παρακαλώ _____	Your passport, please
Την πράσινη κάρτα σας, παρακαλώ _____	Your green card, please
Τον αριθμό κυκλοφορίας σας, _____ παρακαλώ	Your vehicle documents, please
Τη βίζα σας, παρακαλώ_____	Your visa, please
Πού πάτε;_____	Where are you heading?
Πόσο καιρό σκοπεύετε να μείνετε; _____	How long are you planning to stay?
Έχετε τίποτα να δηλώσετε; _____	Do you have anything to declare?
Ανοίξτε αυτό, παρακαλώ _____	Open this, please

My children are entered ___ on this passport	Τα παιδιά μου είναι γραμμένα σ' αυτό το διαβατήριο *ta pedhyámoo íne ghraména saftó to dhiavatírio*
I'm travelling through _____	Είμαι περαστικός/περαστική *íme perastikós/perastikí*
I'm going on vacation to... _	Πηγαίνω για διακοπές σε... *piyéno ya dhiakopés se*
I'm on a business trip _____	Είμαι εδώ για δουλειές *íme edhó ya dhoolyés*
I don't know how long_____ I'll be staying yet	Δεν ξέρω ακόμα πόσο καιρό θα μείνω *dhengxéro akóma póso kyeró tha míno*
I'll be staying here for _____ a weekend	Θα μείνω εδώ ένα Σαββατοκύριακο *tha míno edhó éna savatokíryako*
– for a few days _____	Θα μείνω εδώ λίγες μέρες *tha míno edhó líyes méres*
– for a week_____	Θα μείνω εδώ μία εβδομάδα *tha míno edhó mía evdhomádha*
– for two weeks _____	Θα μείνω εδώ δύο εβδομάδες *tha míno edhó dhío evdhomádhes*
I have nothing to _____ declare	Δεν έχω τίποτα να δηλώσω *dhenécho típota na dhilóso*
I've got...with me_____	Έχω...μαζί μου *écho...mazímoo*

– ...cartons of cigarettes ___ Έχω μία κούτα τσιγάρα μαζί μου
écho mía kóota tsighára mazímoo

– a bottle of... _____ Έχω ένα μπουκάλι... μαζί μου
écho éna bookáli...mazímoo

– some souvenirs _____ Έχω μερικά σουβενίρ μαζί μου
écho meriká soovenír mazímoo

These are personal _____ Αυτά είναι προσωπικά αντικείμενα
effects *aftá íne prosopiká andikímena*

These are not new _____ Αυτά τα πράματα δεν είναι καινούρια
aftá ta prámata dhen íne kenóorya

Here's the receipt _____ Εδώ είναι η απόδειξη
edhó íne i apódhixi

This is for private use _____ Αυτό είναι για προσωπική χρήση
aftó íne ya prosopikí chrísi

How much import duty ____ Πόσο φόρο πρέπει να πληρώσω;
do I have to pay? *póso fóro prépi na pliróso?*

Can I go now? _____ Μπορώ να φύγω τώρα;
boró na fígho tóra?

5 .3 Luggage

Porter! _____ Αχθοφόρε!
achthofóre!

Could you take this _____ Παρακαλώ, πηγαίνετε αυτές τις αποσκευές σε...
luggage to...? *parakaló, piyénete aftés tis aposkevés se...*

How much do I _____ Πόσο σας οφείλω;
owe you? *póso sas ofílo?*

Where can I find a _____ Πού μπορώ να βρω ένα καροτσάκι;
luggage cart? *poo boró na vro éna karotsáki?*

Could you store this _____ Μπορώ να δώσω αυτές τις αποσκευές προς
luggage for me? φύλαξη;
*boró na dhóso aftés tis aposkevés pros
filaxi?*

Where are the luggage ____ Που βρίσκονται οι θυρίδες αποσκευών;
lockers? *poo vrískonde i thirídhes aposkevón?*

I can't get the locker _____ Δεν μπορώ να ανοίξω τη θυρίδα
open *dhemboró na aníxo ti thirídha*

How much is it per item ___ Πόσο κοστίζει το κομμάτι/ τη μέρα;
per day? *póso kostízi to komáti/ti méra?*

This is not my bag/ _____ Αυτή δεν είναι δική μου τσάντα/βαλίτσα
suitcase *aftí dhen íne dhikímoo tsánda/valítsa*

There's one item/bag/ ____ Λείπει ακόμα ένα κομμάτι/μια τσάντα/μια
suitcase missing still βαλίτσα
*lípi akóma éna komáti/mya tsánda/mya
valítsa*

My suitcase is damaged ___ Η βαλίτσα μου έπαθε κάποια ζημιά
i valítsa moo épathe kápya zimyá

ΑΠΑΓΟΡΕΥΕΤΑΙ Η
ΠΡΟΣΠΕΡΑΣΗ
no passing
ΑΠΑΓΟΡΕΥΕΤΑΙ Η
ΣΤΑΘΜΕΥΣΗ
no parking
ΑΡΓΑ
slow
ΑΥΤΟΚΙΝΗΤΟΔΡΟΜΟΣ
road suitable for cars
ΑΦΥΛΑΚΤΗ
ΔΙΑΒΑΣΗ
unmanned crossing
ΔΕΥΤΕΡΕΥΩΝ
ΔΡΟΜΟΣ
minor road
ΔΙΑΧΩΡΙΣΜΟΣ
road divides
ΔΙΟΔΙΑ
toll
ΔΩΣΕΤΕ
ΠΡΟΤΕΡΑΙΟΤΗΤΑ
yield
ΕΘΝΙΚΗ ΟΔΟΣ
(ΜΕ ΔΙΟΔΙΑ)
highway
(with toll)
ΕΙΣΟΔΟΣ
entrance
ΕΛΑΤΤΩΣΑΤΕ
ΤΑΧΥΤΗΤΑ
reduce speed
ΕΛΕΥΘΕΡΗ
ΚΥΚΛΟΦΟΡΙΑ
expressway
ΕΠΑΡΧΙΑΚΗ ΟΔΟΣ
minor road

ΕΠΙΚΙΝΔΥΝΗ
ΔΙΑΣΤΑΥΡΩΣΗ
dangerous inter-
section
ΕΠΙΚΙΝΔΥΝΗ
ΚΑΤΩΦΕΡΕΙΑ
steep hill
ΕΠΙΚΙΝΔΥΝΗ
ΣΤΡΟΦΗ
dangerous curve
ΕΞΟΔΟΣ
exit
ΕΞΟΔΟΣ
ΟΧΗΜΑΤΩΝ
exit for trucks
Η ΤΑΧΥΤΗΤΑ
ΕΛΕΓΧΕΤΑΙ ΜΕ
ΡΑΝΤΑΡ
radar speed checks
ΚΑΤΟΛΙΣΘΗΣΕΙΣ
loose gravel
ΚΕΝΤΡΟ
center
ΚΙΝΔΥΝΟΣ
danger
ΚΛΕΙΣΤΗ ΟΔΟΣ
road closed
ΚΥΚΛΟΦΟΡΙΑ ΑΠΟ
ΑΝΤΙΘΕΤΗ
ΚΑΤΕΥΘΥΝΣΗ
oncoming traffic
ΜΟΝΟΔΡΟΜΟΣ
one-way street
ΝΟΣΟΚΟΜΕΙΟ
hospital

ΟΔΟΣ
ΠΡΟΤΕΡΑΙΟΤΗΤΑΣ
road with priority
over vehicles
entering from side
roads
ΠΑΡΑΚΑΜΠΤΗΡΙΟΣ
diversion
ΠΕΖΟΔΡΟΜΟΣ
pavement
ΠΕΡΙΜΕΝΕΤΕ
wait
ΠΡΟΣΟΧΗ
look out!
ΠΡΟΣ ΠΑΡΑΛΙΑ
to the beach
ΣΤΑΘΜΟΣ ΠΡΩΤΩΝ
ΒΟΗΘΕΙΩΝ
first aid post
ΣΤΕΝΩΜΑ
ΟΔΟΣΤΡΩΜΑΤΟΣ
road narrows
ΣΤΡΟΦΕΣ
curves
ΤΕΛΟΣ
ΑΠΑΓΟΡΕΥΜΕΝΗΣ
ΖΩΝΗΣ
end of forbidden
zone
ΥΨΟΣ
ΠΕΡΙΟΡΙΣΜΕΝΟ
restricted height
ΧΩΜΑΤΟΔΡΟΜΟΣ
packed-earth road

On the road

The parts of a car

(the diagram shows the numbered parts)

1 battery	η μπαταρία	*i bataría*
2 rear light	το πίσω φως	*to píso fos*
3 rear-view mirror	ο καθρέφτης οδηγήσεως	*o kathréftis odhiyíseos*
backup light	το πίσω φανάρι πορείας	*to píso fanári porías*
4 aerial	η αντένα	*i anténa*
car radio	το ραδιόφωνο του	*to radhiófono too*
	αυτοκινήτου	*aftokinítoo*
5 gas tank	το ρεζερβουάρ	*to rezervwár*
6 spark plugs	το μπουζί	*to boozí*
fuel filter	το φίλτρο καυσίμων	*to fíltro kafsímon*
fuel pump	η αντλία καυσίμων	*i andlía kafsímon*
7 side mirror	ο εξωτερικός καθρέφτης	*o exoterikós kathréftis*
8 bumper	ο προφυλακτήρας	*o profilaktíras*
carburetor	το καρμπυρατέρ	*to karbiratér*
crankcase	το κάρτερ	*to kárter*
cylinder	ο κύλινδρος	*o kílindhros*
ignition	οι πλατίνες	*i platínes*
warning light	η λάμπα ελέγχου	*i lámpa elénchoo to*
generator	το δυναμό	*to dhinamó*
accelerator	το πηδάλι γκάζι	*to pidháli too gaz*
handbrake	το χειρόφρενο	*to hiRófreno*
valve	η βαλβίδα	*i valvidha*
9 muffler	ο σιγαστείρας	*o sighastíras*
10 trunk	το πορτμπαγκάζ	*to portbagáz*
11 headlight	ο προβολέας	*o provoléas*
crank shaft	ο στροφαλοφόρος	*o strofalofóros*
12 air filter	το φίλτρο αέρος	*to fíltro aéros*
fog lamp	το πίσω φως ομίχλης	*to píso fos omíchlis*
13 engine block	το σώμα της μηχανής	*to sóma tis mihanís*
camshaft	ο εκκεντροφόρος άξονας	*o ekendrofóros áxonas*
oil filter	το φίλτρο λαδιού	*to fíltro ladhyóo*
oil pump	η αντλία λαδιού	*i andlía ladhyóo*
dipstick	ο δείκτης λαδιού	*o dhíktis ladhyóo*
pedal	το πηδάλι	*to pidháli*
14 door	η πόρτα	*i pórta*
15 radiator	το ψυγείο	*to psiyío*
16 brake disk	ο δίσκος του φρένου	*o dhiskos too fréno*
spare wheel	η ρεσέρβα	*i resérva*
17 indicator	το φλας	*to flas*
18 windshield wiper	ο γυαλοκαθαριστήρας	*o yalokatharistíras*
19 shock absorbers	τα αμορτισέρ	*ta amortisér*
sunroof	η κινητή σκεπή	*i kinití skepí*
starter motor	το στάρτερ	*to stárter*
20 steering column	η στήλη του τιμονιού	*i stíli too timonyóo*
21 exhaust pipe	η εξάτμιση	*i exátmisi*
22 seat belt	η ζώνη ασφαλείας	*i zóni asfalías*
fan	ο ανεμιστήρας	*o anemistíras*
23 distributor	οι αγωγοί διανομής	*i aghoyí dhianomís*
cables	ο λεβιές αλλαγής	
24 gear shift	ταχυτήτων	*io levyés alayís tahitíton*
	το παρμπρίζ	

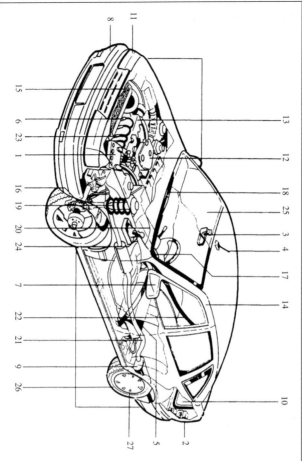

25 windshield water pump	η αντλία νερού	*to parbríz*
26 wheel	η ρόδα	*i andlía neróo*
27 hubcap	το καπάκι της ρόδας	*i ródha*
piston	το έμβολο	*to kapáki tis ródhas*
		to émvolo

5.5 The car

See the diagram on page 49.

● **Particular traffic regulations:**
- **maximum speed** for cars:
100km/h on highways
80km/h outside town centers
50km/h in town centers
- **yield**: all traffic from the right has the right of way.

5.6 The gas station

● **Regular, super and lead-free gas** are all available in Greece, as is diesel. DERV is only permitted in taxis.

How many kilometers to the next gas station, please?	Πόσα χιλιόμετρα είναι ως το πλησιέστερο βενζινάδικο; *pósa hilyómetra íne os to plisiéstero venzinádhiko?*
I would like...liters of..., please	Βάλτε μου... λίτρα *váltemoo...lítra*
– super	Βάλτε μου... λίτρα σούπερ *váltemoo...lítra sóoper*
– leaded	Βάλτε μου... λίτρα απλή βενζίνη *váltemoo...lítra aplí venzíni*
– unleaded	Βάλτε μου... λίτρα ντηζελ *váltemoo...lítra dízel*
– diesel	Βάλτε μου... λίτρα αμόλυβδη *váltemoo...lítra amólivdhi*
I would like...drachmas' worth of gas, please.	Θα ήθελα υγραέριο για... δραχμές *tha íthela ighraéryo ya...dhrachmés*
Fill her up, please	Γεμίστε το, παρακαλώ *yemísteto, parakaló*
Could you check...?	Ελέγξτε το... , παρακαλώ *eléngxte to ... parakaló*
– the oil level	Ελέγξτε το λάδι, παρακαλώ *eléngxte to ládhi, parakaló*
– the tire pressure	Ελέγξτε τα λάστιχα, παρακαλω *eléngxte ta lásticha, parakaló*
Could you change the oil, please?	Μπορείτε να αλλάξετε τα λάδια; *boríte na aláxete ta ládhya?*
Could you clean the windows/the windshield, please?	Μπορείτε να καθαρίσετε τα τζάμια/το παρμπρίζ; *boríte na katharísete ta tzámya/to parbríz?*
Could you wash the car, please?	Μπορείτε να πλύνετε το αυτοκίνητο; *boríte na plínete to aftokínito?*

5.7 Breakdown and repairs

I'm having car trouble Could you give me a hand?	Έπαθα βλάβη. Μπορείτε να με βοηθήσετε; *épatha vlávi. boríte na me voithísete?*
I've run out of gas	Έμεινα από βενζίνη *émina apó venzíni*
I've locked the keys in the car	Έχω αφήσει τα κλειδιά στο αυτοκίνητο *écho afísi ta klidhyá sto aftokínito*

The car/motorcycle/ moped won't start _____	Το αυτοκίνητο/η μοτοσικλέτα/το μηχανάκι δεν παίρνει μπρος *to aftokínito/i motosikléta/to michanáki dhembérni bros*
Could you contact the _____ road service for me, please?	Μπορείτε να τηλεφωνήσετε στην ΕΛΠΑ; *boríte na tilefonísete tin elpá;*
Could you call a garage_____ for me, please?	Μπορείτε να τηλεφωνήσετε σ' ένα γκαράζ; *boríte na tilefonísete séna garáz?*
Could you give me _____ a lift to...?	Μπορείτε να με πάρετε μαζί σας; *boríte na me párete mazísas?*
– a garage/into town?_____	Μπορείτε να με πάτε σ' ένα γκαράζ/στην πόλη; *boríte na me páte séna garáz/stim bóli?*
– a phone booth?_____	Μπορείτε να με πάτε σ' ένα τηλεφωνικό θάλαμο; *boríte na me páte séna tilefonikó thálamo?*
Can we take my _____ bicycle/moped?	Μπορούμε να πάρουμε και το ποδήλατό μου/το μηχανάκι μου; *boróome na pároome kye to podhílatómoo/to michanákimoo*
Could you tow me to _____ a garage?	Μπορείτε να με τραβήξετε σ' ένα γκαράζ; *boríte na me travíxete séna garáz?*
There's probably _____ something wrong with...(See pages 49 and 53)	Πιθανόν να έχει κάτι το... *pithanón na éhi káti to...*
Can you fix it? _____	Μπορείτε να το φτιάξετε; *boríte na to ftyáxete?*
Could you fix my tire? _____	Μπορείτε να κολλήσετε το λάστιχό μου; *boríte na kolísete to lastichómoo?*
Could you change this _____ wheel?	Μπορείτε ν' αλλάξετε αυτή τη ρόδα; *boríte naláxete aftí ti ródha?*
Can you fix it so it'll _____ get me to...?	Μπορείτε να το φτιάξετε για να μπορώ να πάω μέχρι... ; *boríte na to ftyáxete ya na boró na páo méchri...?*
Which garage can _____ help me?	Ποιό γκαράζ μπορεί να με βοηθήσει; *pyo garáz borí na me voithísi?*
When will my car/bicycle _____ be ready?	Πότε θα είναι έτοιμο το αυτοκίνητό μου/το ποδήλατό μου; *póte tha íne étimo to avtokínitómoo/to podhilatómoo?*
Can I wait for it here?_____	Μπορώ να περιμένω εδώ; *boró na periméno edhó?*
How much will it cost? _____	Πόσο θα κοστίσει; *póso tha kostísi?*
Could you confirm the _____ details of the bill?	Μπορείτε να διευκρινήσετε το λογαριασμό; *boríte na dhiefkrinísete to loghariazmó?*
Can I have a receipt for _____ the insurance?	Μπορείτε να μου δώσετε μια απόδειξη για την ασφάλεια; *boríte na moo dhósete mya apódhixi ya tin asfálya?*

The parts of a bicycle
(the diagram shows the numbered parts)

1 rear light	το πίσω φως	to píso fos
2 rear wheel	η πισινή ρόδα	i pisiní rhódha
3 (luggage) carrier	η σχάρα	i schára
4 bicycle fork	η κεφαλή διχαλωτού άξονος	i kefalí dhichalotóo áxonos
5 bell	το κουδούνι	to koodhóoni
tire	το λάστιχο	to lásticho
6 crank	η μανιβέλα	i manivéla
7 gear change	η αλλαγή ταχυτήτων	i alayí tahitíton
wire	το συρματάκι	to sirmatáki
generator	το δυναμό	to dhinamó
bicycle trailer	το ποδήλατο με ρυμουλκούμενο καροτσάκι	to podhílato me rimoolkóomeno karotsáki
frame	ο σκελετός	o skeletós
8 dress guard	ο προφυλακτήρας φορεμάτων	o profilaktíras foremáton
9 chain guard	η αλυσίδα	i alisídha
chain lock	η αλυσίδα (για το κλείδωμα του ποδηλάτου)	i alisídha (ya to klídhoma too podhilátoo)
odometer	το κοντέρ	o kontér
child's seat	η παιδική σέλα	i pedhikí séla
10 headlight	το φανάρι	to fanári
bulb	η λάμπα	i lámpa
11 pedal	το πηδάλι	to pidháli
12 pump	η τρόμπα	i trómba
13 reflector	ο πίσω αντανακλαστήρας	o píso andanaklistíras
14 brake shoe	το τακάκι	to takáki
15 brake cable	το καλώδιο του φρένου	to kalódhyo too frénoo
16 ring lock	η κυκλική κλειδαριά	i kiklikí klidharyá
17 carrier straps	τα λουριά της σχάρας	ta looryá tis scháras
tachometer	το ταχύμετρο	to tahímetro
18 spoke	η ακτίνα της ρόδας	i aktína tis ródhas
19 mudguard	το φτερό	o fteró
20 handlebar	το τιμόνι	to timóni
21 chain wheel	η ρόδα της αλυσίδας	i ródha tis alisídhas
22 crank axle	ο άξονας του πηδαλιού	too pidhalyóo áxonas
rim	η ζάντα	i zánda
23 valve	η αεροβαλβίδα	i aerovalvídha
24 valve tube	το σωληνάκι της αεροβαλβίδας	to solináki tis aerovalvidhas
25 gear cable	το καλώδιο επιτάχυνσης	to kalódhyo epitáchinsis
26 front fork	η μπροστινή φουρκέτα	i brostiní foorkéta
27 front wheel	η μπροστινή ρόδα	i brostiní ródha
28 seat	η σέλα	i séla

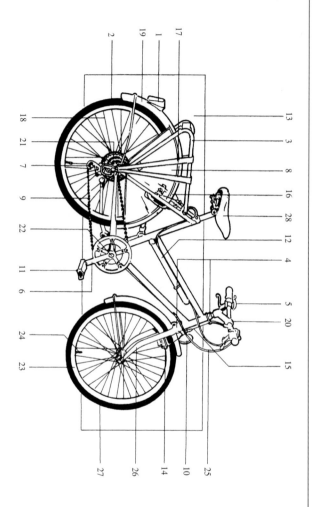

5.8 The bicycle/moped

See the diagram on page 53.

● **Bicycle paths** are non-existent in Greece, and little consideration for cyclists is shown on the roads. In tourist places bikes and mopeds can be rented at tourist centers. The maximum speed for mopeds is 40km/h, both inside and outside town centers. Passengers may only be carried on small motorcycles clearly designed with a passenger seat. A crash helmet is advisable.

Δεν έχω ανταλλακτικά για το_____ αυτοκίνητό σας/το ποδήλατό σας	I don't have parts for your car/bicycle
Πρέπει να πάρω τα ανταλλακτικά από ____ κάπου αλλού	I have to get the parts from somewhere else
Πρέπει να παραγγείλω τα_____ ανταλλακτικά	I have to order the parts
Αυτό θέλει μισή μέρα _____	That'll take half a day
Αυτό θέλει μια μέρα _____	That'll take a day
Αυτό θέλει μερικές μέρες _____	That'll take a few days
Αυτό θέλει μια εβδομάδα _____	That'll take a week
Το αυτοκίνητό σας είναι εντελώς _____ διαλυμένο	Your car is a write-off
Δεν μπορούμε να κάνουμε τίποτα πια ____	It can't be repaired
Το αυτοκίνητο/η μοτοσικλέτα/το _____ μηχανάκι/το ποδήλατο είναι έτοιμο στις...	The car/motorcycle/ moped/bicycle will be ready at... o'clock

5.9 Renting a vehicle

I'd like to rent a..._____	Θα ήθελα να νοικιάσω ένα... *tha íthela na nikyáso éna...*
Do I need a (special)_____ license for that?	Χρειάζομαι μια (ορισμένη) άδεια οδηγήσεως γι' αυτό; *chriázome mya (orizméni) ádhya odhiyíseos yavtó?*
I'd like to rent the...for... ___	Θέλω να νοικιάσω το... για... *thélo na nikyáso to...ya...*
– one day _____	Θέλω να νοικιάσω το... για μία μέρα *thélo na nikyáso to...ya mía méra*
– two days _____	Θέλω να νοικιάσω το... για δύο μέρες *thélo na nikyáso to...ya dhío méres*
How much is that per_____ day/week?	Πόσο κάνει την ημέρα/την εβδομάδα; *póso káni tin iméra/tin evdhomádha?*
How much is the _____ deposit?	Πόσο είναι η εγγύηση; *póso íne i engíisi?*
Could I have a receipt ____ for the deposit?	Μπορείτε να μου δώσετε μια απόδειξη ότι πλήρωσα την εγγύηση; *boríte ne moo dhósete mya apódhixi óti plírosa tin engíisi?*
How much is the _____ surcharge per kilometer?	Πόσο είναι το συμπληρωματικό ποσό για κάθε χιλιόμετρο; *póso íne to simbliromatikó posó ya káthe hilyómetro?*

Does that include gas?	Είναι αυτό μαζί με τη βενζίνη;	íne aftó mazí me ti venzíni?
Does that include insurance?	Είναι αυτό μαζί με την ασφάλεια;	íne aftó mazí me tin asfálya?
What time can I pick the...up tomorrow?	Τι ώρα μπορώ να περάσω αύριο να πάρω το...;	ti óra boró na peráso ávrio na páro to...?
When does the...have to be back?	Πότε πρέπει να επιστρέψω το... ;	póte prépi na epistrépso to...?
Where's the gas tank?	Πού βρίσκεται το ρεζερβουάρ;	poo vrískete to rezervvár?
What sort of fuel does it take?	Τι είδος καύσιμα χρειάζεται;	ti ídhos káfsima chriázete?

⑤ .10 Hitchhiking

Where are you heading?	Πού πηγαίνετε;	poo piyénete?
Can I come along?	Μπορείτε να με πάρετε μαζί σας;	boríte na me párete mazísas?
Can my boyfriend/ girlfriend come too?	Μπορείτε να πάρετε και το φίλο μου/τη φίλη μου;	boríte na párete kye to fílomoo/ti fílimoo?
I'm trying to get to...	Εγώ πηγαίνω σε...	eghó piyéno se...
Is that on the way to...?	Βρίσκεται αυτό στο δρόμο για...	vrískete aftó sto dhrómo ya...
Could you drop me off...?	Μπορείτε να με αφήσετε σε... ;	boríte na me afísete se...?
– here?	Μπορείτε να με αφήσετε εδώ;	boríte na me afísete edhó?
– at the exit for...?	Μπορείτε να με αφήσετε στην έξοδο για... ;	boríte na me afísete stin éxodho ya...?
– in the center?	Μπορείτε να με αφήσετε στο κέντρο;	boríte na me afísete sto kéndro?
– at the next rotary?	Μπορείτε να με αφήσετε στην επόμενη ροτόντα;	boríte na me afísete stin epómeni
Could you stop here, please?	Μπορείτε να σταματήσετε εδώ, παρακαλώ;	boríte na stamatísete edhó, parakaló?
I'd like to get out here	Θέλω να κατεβώ εδώ	thélo na katevó edhó
Thanks for the lift	Ευχαριστώ για την εξυπηρέτηση	efcharistó ya tin exipirétisi

Public transportation

Public transportation

6.1 **I**n general

Announcements

Το τρένο για..., που φεύγει στις...έχει _____ καθυστέρηση...λεπτών	The...train to...has been delayed by...minutes
Στη γραμμή...φτάνει τώρα το _____ τρένο για.../από...	The train now arriving at platform...is the...train to.../from...
Στη γραμμή...βρίσκεται ακόμα το _____ τρένο για...	The...train for...is still at platform...
Το τρένο για...φεύγει σήμερα από _____ την πλατφόρμα...	Today the...train to...is due to leave from platform...
Φτάνουμε τώρα στο σταθμό... _____	We're now approaching...

Where does this train _____ go to?	Πού πηγαίνει αυτό το τρένο; *poo piyéni aftó to tréno?*
Does this boat go to...? ____	Αυτό το πλοίο πηγαίνει σε...; *aftó to plío piyéni se ...?*
Can I take this bus to...? ___	Μπορώ να πάω σε...με το λεωφορείο; *boró na páo se ... me to leoforío?*
Does this train stop at...? __	Αυτό το τρένο σταματάει σε...; *aftó to tréno stamatái se ...?*
Is this seat taken/free/ _____ reserved?	Αυτή η θέση είναι πιασμένη/ελεύθερη/κλεισμένη; *aftí i thési íne pyazméni/eléftheri/klizméni?*
I've reserved... _____	Έχω κλείσι... *écho klísi ...*
Could you tell me _____ where I have to get off for...?	Μου λέτε πού πρέπει να κατεβώ για...; *moo léte poo prépi na katevó ya...?*
Could you let me _____ know when we get to...?	Μπορείτε να με προειδοποιήσετε όταν θα φτάνουμε κοντά σε...; *boríte na me proidhopiísete ótan tha ftánoome kondá se...?*
Could you stop at the _____ next stop, please?	Μπορείτε να σταματήσετε στην επόμενη στάση, παρακαλώ; *boríte na stamtísete stin epómeni stási, parakaló?*
Where are we now? _____	Πού είμαστε εδώ; *poo ímaste edhó?*
Do I have to get off here? __	Πρέπει να κατεβώ εδώ; *prépi na katevó edhó?*
Have we already _____ passed...?	Περάσαμε κιόλας...; *perásame kyólas...?*
How long have I_____ been asleep?	Πόση ώρα κοιμήθηκα; *pósi óra kimíthika?*
How long does_____ the...stop here?	Πόση ώρα κάνει στάση εδώ το... ; *pósi óra káni stási edhó to...?*

.2 Questions to passengers

Ticket types

Πρώτη ή δεύτερη θέση;_____	First or second class?
Απλό εισιτήριο ή με επιστροφή;_____	Single or return?
Καπνίζοντες ή μη καπνίζοντες;_____	Smoking or nonsmoking?
Στο παράθυρο ή στο διάδρομο;_____	Window or aisle?
Μπροστά ή πίσω;_____	Front or back?
Απλή θέση ή κουκέτα;_____	Seat or berth?
Πάνω, στη μέση ή κάτω;_____	Top, middle or bottom?
Τουριστική θέση ή μπιζνεσκλάς _____	Tourist class or business class?
Καμπίνα ή απλή θέση;_____	Cabin or seat?
Για ένα ή δύο άτομα;_____	Single or double?
Με πόσα άτομα ταξιδεύετε;_____	How many are traveling?

.3 Tickets

Can I come back on _____ the same ticket?	Είναι με επιστροφή αυτό το εισιτήριο; *íne me epistrofí aftó to isitírio?*
Can I change on_____ this ticket?	Μπορώ να συνεχίσω μ' αυτό το εισιτήριο; *boró na sinechíso maftó to isitírio?*
How long is this ticket _____ valid for?	Για πόσο καιρό ισχύει αυτό το εισιτήριο; *ya póso kyeró ischíi aftó to isitírio?*
Where can I...? _____	Πού μπορώ να... ; *poo boró na...?*
- buy a ticket? _____	Πού μπορώ να αγοράσω εισιτήριο; *poo boró na aghoráso isitírio?*
- make a reservation?_____	Πού μπορώ να κλείσω θέση; *poo boró na klíso thési?*
- reserve a flight?_____	Πού μπορώ να κλείσω θέση στο αεροπλάνο; *poo boró na klíso thési sto aeropláno?*
Could I have a...to...,_____ please?	Θέλω ένα...για... *thélo éna...ya...*
- a single _____	Θέλω ένα απλό εισιτήριο για... *thélo éna apló isitírio ya...*
- a return _____	Θέλω ένα μετ επιστροφής για... *thélo éna metepistrofís ya...*
first class _____	πρώτη θέση *próti thési*
second class _____	δεύτερη θέση *dhéfteri thési*
tourist class_____	τουριστική θέση *tooristikí thési*
business class _____	μπιζνεσκλάς *biznesklás*
I'd like to reserve a _____ seat/berth/cabin	Θέλω να κλείσω θέση/κρεβάτι/καμπίνα *thélo na klíso thési/kreváti/kabína*
I'd like to reserve a berth __ in the sleeping car	Θέλω να κλείσω θέση στο βαγκον-λί *thélo na klíso thési sto vagonlí*
top/middle/bottom _____	πάνω/στη μέση/κάτω *páno/sti mési/káto*

Destination

Πού πηγαίνετε; _____	Where are you traveling to?
Πότε φεύγετε; _____	When are you leaving?
Το...σας φεύγει στις... _____	Your...leaves at...
Πρέπει ν' αλλάξετε τρένο _____	You have to change trains
Πρέπει να κατεβείτε σε... _____	You have to get off at...
Πρέπει να πάτε μέσω... _____	You have to travel via...
Η αναχώρηση είναι τη... _____	The outward journey is on...
Η επιστροφή είναι τη... _____	The return journey is on...
Πρέπει να επιβιβαστείτε στις... το _____ αργότερο	You have to be on board by...

Inside the vehicle

Το εισιτήριό σας, παρακαλώ _____	Your ticket, please
Τη βεβαίωση της κράτησης, παρακαλώ ___	Your reservation, please
Το διαβατήριό σας, παρακαλώ _____	Your passport, please
Κάθεστε σε λάθος θέση _____	You're in the wrong seat
Βρίσκεσθε σε λάθος... _____	You're on/in the wrong...
Αυτή η θέση είναι κλεισμένη _____	This seat is reserved
Πρέπει να πληρώσετε συμπληρωματικό ποσό	You'll have to pay an extra charge
Το... έχει καθυστέρηση... λεπτών _____	The...has been delayed by...minutes

smoking/no smoking _____ καπνίζοντες/μη καπνίζοντες
kapnízondes/mi kapnízondes

by the window _____ στο παράθυρο
sto paráthiro

single/double _____ για ένα άτομο/ για δύο άτομα
ya éna átomo/ya dhío átoma

at the front/back_____ μπροστά/πίσω
brostá/píso

There are...of us_____ Είμαστε...άτομα
ímaste...átoma

with a car_____ Μ' ένα αυτοκίνητο
ména avtokínito

with a trailer _____ Μ' ένα τροχόσπιτο
ména trochóspito

with ... bicycles _____ Με .. ποδήλατα
me...podhílata

Do you also have...? _____ Μήπως έχετε και...;
mípos éhete ke...?

– season tickets? _____ Μήπως έχετε και κάρτα πολλαπλών
διαδρομών;
mípos éhete ke kárta polaplón dhiadhromón?

– weekly tickets? _____ Μήπως έχετε και κάρτα για μια εβδομάδα;
mípos éhete ke kárta ya mya evdhomáda?

– monthly tickets? _____ Μήπως έχετε και κάρτα για ένα μήνα;
mípos éhete ke kárta ya éna mína?

Public transportation

6

Where's...?	Πού είναι...;
	poo íne...?
Where's the information desk?	Πού είναι το γραφείο πληροφοριών;
	poo íne to ghrafío pliroforyón?
Where can I find a timetable?	Πού είναι ο πίνακας αφίξεων/αναχωρήσεων;
	poo íne o pínakas afíxeon/anachoríseon?
Where's the...desk?	Πού είναι η θυρίδα για...
	poo íne i thirídha ya...?
Do you have a city map with the bus/the subway routes on it?	Μήπως έχετε ένα χάρτη της πόλης με το δίκτυο λεωφορείων/του μετρό;
	mípos éhete éna chárti tis pólis me to dhíktio leoforíon/too metró?
Do you have a timetable?	Μήπως έχετε το ωράριο των δρομολογίων;
	mípos éhete to orário ton dhromoloyíon?
I'd like to confirm/ cancel/change my reservation for/trip to...	Θέλω να επιβεβαιώσω/ακυρώσω/αλλάξω την κράτησή μου/το ταξίδι μου σε...
	thélo na epiveveóso/akiróso/aláxo tingrátisímoo/to taxídhi moo se...
Will I get my money back?	Θα πάρω πίσω τα λεφτά μου;
	tha páro píso ta leftá moo?
I want to go to... How do I get there?	Πρέπει να πάω σε ... Πώς πάω εκεί το γρηγορότερο;
	prépi na páo se ... Pos páo ekí to ghrighorótero?
How much is a single/return to...?	Πόσο κάνει ένα απλό εισιτήριο/ένα μετ' επιστροφής;
	póso káni éna apló isitírio/éna metepistrofís?
Do I have to pay an extra charge?	Πρέπει να πληρώσω συμπληρωματικό εισιτήριο;
	prépi na pliróso simbliromatikó isitírio?
Can I interrupt my journey with this ticket?	Μπορώ να διακόψω το ταξίδι μου μ' αυτό το εισιτήριο;
	boró na dhiakópso to taxídhimoo maftó to isitírio?
How much luggage am I allowed?	Πόσες αποσκευές μπορώ να πάρω μαζί μου;
	póses aposkevés boró na páro mazímoo?
Does this...travel direct?	Αυτό το...πηγαίνει κατ' ευθείαν;
	aftó to...piyéni katefthían?
Do I have to change trains/buses/boats? Where?	Πρέπει ν' αλλάξω τρένο/λεωφορείο/πλοίο; Πού;
	prépi naláxo tréno/leoforío/plío? Poo?
Does the plane touch down anywhere en route?	Το αεροπλάνο κάνει ενδιάμεσες προσγειώσεις;
	to aeropláno káni endhiámeses prosyiósis?
Does the boat stop at any ports on the way?	Το πλοίο πιάνει σκάλα και σ' άλλα λιμάνια;
	to plío pyáni skála ke sáala limánya?
Does the train/ bus stop at...?	Το τρένο/το λεωφορείο κάνει στάση σε...;
	to tréno/to leoforío káni stási se...?
Where should I get off?	Πού πρέπει να κατεβώ;
	poo prépi na katevó?
Is there a connection to...?	Υπάρχει ανταπόκριση για ...
	ipárchi andapókrisi ya...
How long do I have to wait?	Πόση ώρα πρέπει να περιμένω;
	pósi óra prépi na periméno?
When does...leave?	Πότε φεύγει...;
	póte févyi...?

What time does the _____ first/last/next...leave?	Τι ώρα φεύγει το πρώτο/τελευταίο/επόμενο...; *ti óra févyi to próto/teleftéo/epómeno...?*
How long does...take? _____	Πόση ώρα κάνει το...; *pósi óra káni to...?*
What time does...arrive _____ in...?	Τι ώρα φτάνει το...σε...; *ti óra ftáni to...se...?*
Where does the...to... _____ leave from?	Από πού φεύγει το...για...; *apó poo févyi to...ya...?*
Is this...to...? _____	Αυτό είναι το...για...; *aftó íne to...ya....?Δ·b!*

.5 Airplanes

● **In addition to** scheduled flights from the US to Athens and Thessaloniki there are a large number of charters to both cities and to Corfu, Kos, Crete and Rhodes. Athens has two airports, one for Olympic Airways and one for other airlines; the two airports are quite close to one another. They have two areas, *αφίξεις* (arrivals) and *αναχωρήσεις* (departures). At the check-in desk you will receive a *δελτίο επιβασάξεως* (boarding card) and will be told which *έξοδος* (gate) you will be leaving from.

In a Greek airport you will find the following signs:

αναχωρήσεις **departures**	εσωτερικές **internal/domestic**	πτήσεις εξωτερικού **international flights**
αφίξεις **arrivals**	ανταποκρίσεις **connecting flights**	πτήσεις εσωτερικού **domestic flights**

.6 Trains

● **The rail network** in Greece is not very extensive, but rail travel is generally much cheaper than in the US. The Greek State Railways company is responsible for the line from Thessaloniki to Athens. Much of the route is single track, and there are innumerable small stations. Another company runs the loop of track from Athens around the Peloponnese. You can travel first or second class, and students, children and groups of more than ten persons can obtain reductions. It is advisable to reserve a seat at the time you purchase your ticket.

.7 Taxis

● **There are plenty** of taxis in Greece and they are usually much cheaper than in the US. In Athens and Thessaloniki taxis act rather like buses; they pick up and drop off passengers en route. Virtually all taxis have a meter, but it is often possible to agree a price for a longer trip in advance. An additional charge is usual for luggage, a journey at night, on a Sunday or public holiday, or to an airport.

Taxi! _____	ταξί *taxí!*
Could you get me a taxi, _____ please?	Μπορείτε να καλέσετε ένα ταξί για μένα; *boríte na kalésete éna taxí ya ména?*
Where can I find a taxi _____ around here?	Πού μπορώ να βρω ένα ταξί εδώ κοντά; *poo boró na vro éna taxí edhó kondá?*

Public transportation

ελεύθερο	κατειλημμένο	σταθμός ταξί
free	taken	taxi stand

Could you take me to..., please?
Με πηγαίνετε σε..., παρακαλώ;
me piyénete se..., parakaló?

– this address
Με πηγαίνετε σ' αυτή τη διεύθυνση, παρακαλώ;
me piyénete saftí ti dhiéfthinsi, parakaló?

– the...hotel
Με πηγαίνετε στο ξενοδοχείο..., παρακαλώ;
me piyénete sto xenodhohío..., parakaló?

– the town/center of the city
Με πηγαίνετε στο κέντρο, παρακαλώ;
me piyénete sto kéndro, parakaló?

– the station
Με πηγαίνετε στο σταθμό, παρακαλώ;
me piyénete sto stathmó, parakaló?

– the airport
Με πηγαίνετε στο αεροδρόμιο, παρακαλώ;
me piyénete sto aerodhrómio, parakaló?

How much is the trip to...?
Πόσο κάνει η διαδρομή μέχρι...;
póso káni i dhiadromí méchri...?

How far is it to...?
Πόσο μακριά είναι μέχρι... ;
póso makriá íne méchri...?

Could you turn on the meter, please?
Μπορείτε να βάλετε το μετρητή, παρακαλώ;
boríte na válete to metrití, parakaló?

I'm in a hurry
Βιάζομαι
vyázome

Could you speed up/slow down a little?
Μπορείτε να πηγαίνετε πιο γρήγορα/πιο αργά, παρακαλώ;
boríte na piyénete pyo ghríghora/pyo arghá, parakaló?

Could you take a different route?
Μπορείτε να πάρετε ένα άλλο δρόμο;
boríte na párete éna álo dhrómo?

I'd like to get out here, please
Αφήστε με να κατεβώ εδώ, παρακαλώ
afíste me na katevó edhó, parakaló

You have to go...here
Εδώ πρέπει να πάτε...
edhó prépi na páte...

You have to go straight here
Εδώ πρέπει να πάτε ίσια
edhó prépi na páte ísya

You have to turn left here
Εδώ πρέπει να πάτε αριστερά
edhó prépi na páte aristerá

You have to turn right here
Εδώ πρέπει να πάτε δεξιά
edhó prépi na páte dhexyá

This is it
Εδώ είναι
edhó íne

Could you wait a minute for me, please?
Μπορείτε να με περιμένετε ένα λεπτό;
boríte na me periménete éna leptó?

7

Overnight accommodation

Overnight accommodation

7 **.1 G**eneral

● **Hotel accommodation:** hotels (ξενοδοχεία) are in different categories: luxury class, A class, B class, C class, D class, and E class. The classification is somewhat arbitrary, and it is always worth trying a cheap hotel. An expensive hotel will not necessarily be more pleasant or comfortable than a cheaper one.
Most hotels serve breakfast.

Rooms in private houses or pensions are available and offer a cheap and interesting form of accommodation. This is the best way to get to know Greeks. The tourist police can supply you with a list of rooms available in a particular place.

Motels are rare in Greece; they are only to be found close to the highways.

Youth Hostels exist in the cities; they are divided into male and female sections.

Camping sites are regulated by the Greek National Tourist office (EOT). They are divided into three price levels. There are many sites along the coasts, but they are rarer inland. It is not legal to camp outside such sites.

Πόσο καιρό θέλετε να μείνετε; _____	How long will you be staying?
Μπορείτε να συμπληρώσετε αυτό _____ το έντυπο, παρακαλώ	Fill out this form, please
Το διαβατήριό σας, παρακαλώ _____	Could I see your passport?
Πρέπει να πληρώσετε εγγύηση _____	I'll need a deposit
Πρέπει να προπληρώσετε_____	You'll have to pay in advance

My name's...I've made _____ a reservation over the phone/by mail	Το όνομά μου είναι...Έκλεισα (τηλεφωνικώς/γραπτά) μια θέση *to ónomámoo íne ... éklisa (tilefonikós/ghraptá) mya thési*
How much is it per _____ night/week/ month?	Πόσο κάνει τη νύχτα/την εβδομάδα/το μήνα; *póso káni ti níchta/tin evdhomádha/to mína?*
We'll be staying at _____ least...nights/weeks	Θα μείνουμε τουλάχιστον...νύχτες/εβδομάδες *tha mínoome toolάchiston...níchtes/evdhomádhes*
We don't know yet _____	Δεν ξέρουμε ακόμα ακριβώς *dhen xéroome akóma akrivós*
Do you allow pets _____ (cats/dogs)?	Επιτρέπονται τα κατοικίδια ζώα; *epitréponde ta katikídhia zóa?*
What time does the _____ gate/door open/close?	Τι ώρα κλείνει/ανοίγει η εξώπορτα/η πόρτα; *ti óra klíni/aníyi i exόporta/i pórta?*
Could you get me a taxi, _____ please?	Μου φωνάζετε ένα ταξί, παρακαλώ; *moo fonázete éna taxí, parakaló?*
Where's the manager? _____	Πού είναι ο διαχειριστής; *poo íne o dhiahiristís?*

.2 Camping

See the diagram on page 67.

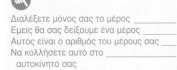

Διαλέξετε μόνος σας το μέρος _____	You can pick your own site
Εμείς θα σας δείξουμε ένα μέρος _____	You'll be allocated a site
Αυτός είναι ο αριθμός του μέρους σας ___	This is your site number
Να κολλήσετε αυτό στο _____ αυτοκίνητό σας	Stick this on your car, please
Να μην χάσετε αυτή την κάρτα _____	Please don't lose this card

Are we allowed to _____ camp here?	Μπορούμε να κατασκηνώσουμε εδώ; *boróome na kataskinósoome edhó?*
There are...of us and _____ ...tents	Είμαστε...άτομα και...σκηνές *ímaste...átoma ke...skinés*
Can we pick our _____ own site?	Μπορούμε να διαλέξουμε μόνοι μας ένα μέρος; *boróome na dhialéxoome mónimas éna méros?*
Do you have a quiet _____ spot for us?	Έχετε ένα ήσυχο μέρος για μας; *éhete éna isicho méros ya mas?*
Do you have any other ___ sites available?	Δεν έχετε ένα άλλο μέρος ελεύθερο; *dhen éhete éna álo méros eléfthero?*
It's too windy/sunny/ _____ shady here	Έχει πολύ αέρα/ήλιο/ίσκιο εδώ *éhi polí aéra/ílyo/ískyo edhó*
It's too crowded here _____	Έχει πολλή κίνηση εδώ *éhi polí kínisi edhó*
The ground's too _____ hard/uneven	Το έδαφος είναι πολύ σκληρό/άνισο *to édhafos íne polí skliró/ániso*
Do you have a level _____ spot for the camper/trailer/folding trailer?	Έχετε ένα ίσιο μέρος για το κάμπερ μας/το τροχόσπιτο μας. το λυόμενο τροχόσπιτό μας; *éhete éna ísyo méros ya to kámpermas/to trochóspitomas /to liómeno trochóspitomas*
Could we have adjoining __ sites?	Μπορούμε να κατασκηνώσουμε δίπλα-δίπλα; *boróome na kataskinósoome dhípla-dhípla?*
Can we park the car _____ next to the tent?	Μπορώ να παρκάρω το αυτοκίνητο δίπλα στη σκηνή; *boró na parkáro to aftokínito dhípla sti skiní?*
How much is it per _____ person/tent/trailer/car?	Πόσο κάνει το άτομο/για μία σκηνή/για ένα τροχόσπιτο/για ένα αυτοκίνητο; *póso káni to átomo/ya mía skiní/ya éna trochóspito/ya éna aftokínito?*
Are there any chalets to ___ rent?	Νοικιάζονται καλύβες; *nikyázonde kalíves?*
Are there any...? _____	Υπάρχουν εδώ...; *ipárchoon edhó...?*
– any hot showers? _____	Υπάρχουν εδώ ντους με ζεστό νερό *ipárchoon edhó doos me zestó neró*
– washing machines? _____	Υπάρχουν εδώ πλυντήρια; *ipárchoon edhó plindíria?*
Is there a...on the site? _____	Υπάρχει σ' αυτό το χώρο...; *ipárchi saftó to chóro...?*
Is there a children's _____ play area on the site?	Υπάρχει σ' αυτό το χώρο μια παιδική χαρά; *ipárchi saftó to chóro mya pedhikí chará?*

Overnight accommodation

Camping equipment
(the diagram shows the numbered parts)

luggage space	ο χώρος αποσκευών	*o chóros aposkevón I*
can opener	το ανοιχτήρι	*to anichtíri*
butane gas bottle	η μποτίλια υγραερίου	*i botílya ighraeríoo*
1 pannier	η τσάντα του ποδηλάτου	*i tsánda too podilátoo*
2 gas cooker	η κουζίνα υγραερίου	*i koozína ighraeríoo*
3 groundsheet	το πάτωμα της σκηνής	*to pátoma tis skinís*
hammer	το σφυρί	*to sfirí*
hammock	η μπράντα	*i bránda*
4 gas can	το μπιντόνι	*to bidóni*
campfire	η πυρά	*i pirá*
5 folding chair	η πτυσσόμενη καρέκλα	*i ptisómeni karékla*
6 insulated picnic box	η τσάντα-ψυγείο	*i tsánda-psiyío*
ice pack	ο ψυκτήρας	*o psiktíras*
compass	η πυξίδα	*i pixídha*
wick	το φυτίλι	*to fitíli*
corkscrew	το τιρμπουσόν	*to tirboosón*
7 airbed	το αερόστρωμα	*to aeróstroma*
8 airbed plug	το βούλωμα του αεροστρώματος	*to vóoloma too aerostrómatos*
pump	το ποδοκίνητο φυσερό	*to podhokinitó fiseró*
9 awning	το προστέγασμα της σκηνής	*to prostéghazma tis skinís*
10 mat	το χαλάκι	*to chaláki*
11 pan	η κατσαρόλα	*i katsaróla*
12 pan handle	το χερούλι	*to heróoli*
primus stove	η γκαζιέρα	*i gazyéra*
zipper	το φερμουάρ	*to fermwár*
13 backpack	το σακίδιο	*to sakídhyo*
14 guy rope	το σχοινί της σκηνής	*to schiní tis skinís*
sleeping bag	ο υπνόσακος	*o ipnósekos*
15 storm lantern	η λάμπα θύελλας	*i lámpa thíelas*
camp bed	το ράντζο	*to rántso*
table	το τραπέζι	*to trapézi*
16 tent	η σκηνή	*i skiní*
17 tent peg	το πασαλάκι της σκηνής	*to pasaláki tis skinís*
18 tent pole	ο ορθοστάτης της σκηνής	*o orthostátis tis skinís*
vacuum	το θερμός	*to thermós*
19 water bottle	το παγούρι	*to paghóori*
clothespin	το μανταλάκι	*to mandaláki*
clothesline	το σχοινί της μπουγάδας	*to schiní tis booghádhas*
windbreak	ο ανεμοφράκτης	*o anemofráktis*
20 flashlight	ο φακός	*o fakós*
pocket knife	ο σουγιάς	*o sooyás*

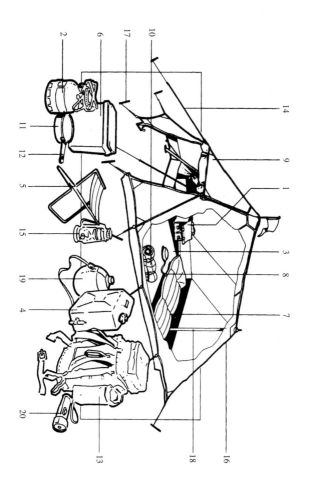

Are there covered cooking facilities on the site?	Υπάρχει σκεπαστός χώρος για μαγείρεμα; *ipárchi skepastós chóros ya mayírevma?*
Can I rent a safe here?	Μπορώ να νοικιάσω ένα χρηματοκιβώτιο; *boró na nikyáso éna chrimatokivótyo?*
Are we allowed to barbecue here?	Επιτρέπεται εδώ το μπάρμπεκιου; *epitrépete edhó to barbekyóo?*
Are there any power outlets?	Υπάρχουν ηλεκτρικές συνδέσεις; *ipárchoon ilektrikés sindhésis?*
Is there drinking water?	Υπάρχει πόσιμο νερό; *ipárchi pósimo neró?*
When's the garbage collected?	Πότε μαζεύουν τα σκουπίδια; *póte mazévoon ta skoopídhya?*
Do you sell gas bottles (butane gas/propane gas)?	Πουλάτε φιάλες υγραερίου (πετρογκάζ); *pooláte fyáles ighraeríoo (petrogáz)?*

.3 Hotel/B&B/apartment/holiday rental

Do you have a single/double room available?	Έχετε ένα ελεύθερο μονό/διπλό δωμάτιο; *éhete éna eléfthero monó/dhipló dhomátyo?*
per person/per room	το άτομο/το δωμάτιο *to átomo/to dhomátyo*
Does that include breakfast/lunch/dinner?	Με το πρωινό/το μεσημεριανό/το βραδινό; *me to proinó/to mesimeryanó/to vradhinó?*
Could we have two adjoining rooms?	Μπορούμε να έχουμε δύο δωμάτια δίπλα-δίπλα; *boróome na échoome dhío dhomátya dhípla-dhípla?*
with/without toilet/bath/shower	με/χωρίς τουαλέτα/μπάνιο/ντους *me/chorís twaléta/bányo/doos*
(not) facing the street	(όχι) από την μεριά του δρόμου *(óhi) apó ti meryá too dhrómou*
with/without a view of the sea	με/χωρίς θέα προς τη θάλασσα *me/chorís théa pros ti thálasa*
Is there...in the hotel?	Το ξενοδοχείο έχει...; *to xenodhohío éhi...?*
Is there an elevator in the hotel	Το ξενοδοχείο έχει ασανσέρ; *to xenodhohío éhi asansér?*
Do you have room service?	Το ξενοδοχείο έχει εξυπηρέτηση δωματίου/ρουμ σέρβις; *to xenodhohío éhi exipirétisi dhomatíoo/room sérvis*
Could I see the room?	Μπορώ να δω το δωμάτιο; *boró na dho to dhomátyo?*
I'll take this room	Θα πάρω αυτό το δωμάτιο *tha páro aftó to dhomátyo*
We don't like this one	Αυτό το δωμάτιο δε μας αρέσει *aftó to dhomátyo dhe mas arési*
Do you have a larger/less expensive room?	Έχετε ένα μεγαλύτερο/πιο φτηνό δωμάτιο; *éhete éna meghalítero/pyo ftinó dhomátyo?*
Could you put in a cot?	Μπορείτε να βάλετε κι ένα παιδικό κρεβάτι στο δωμάτιό μας; *boríte na válete kyéna pedhikó kreváti sto dhomátiómas?*
What time's breakfast?	Τί ώρα είναι το πρωινό; *ti óra íne to proinó?*

Where's the dining room?	Πού είναι η τραπεζαρία;
	poo íne i trapezaría?
Can I have breakfast in my room?	Μπορώ να έχω το πρωινό στο δωμάτιό μου;
	boró na écho to proinó sto dhomátiómoo?
Where's the emergency exit/fire escape?	Πού είναι η έξοδος κινδύνου ή η σκάλα πυρκαγιάς;
	poo íne i éxodhos kindhínoo/i skála pirkayás?

Η τουαλέτα και το ντους είναι _____ στον ίδιο όροφο/στο δωμάτιό σας	You can find the toilet and shower on the same floor/in the room
Από δω, παρακαλώ _____	This way, please
Το δωμάτιό σας είναι στο...όροφο, _____ ο αριθμός είναι...	Your room is on the...floor, number...

Where can I park my car (safely)?	Υπάρχει ένα (ασφαλές) μέρος όπου μπορώ να παρκάρω το αυτοκίνητό μου;
	ipárchi éna (asfalés) méros ópoo boró na parkáro to aftokínitómoo?
The key to room..., please	Το κλειδί του δωματίου..., παρακαλώ
	to klidhí too dhomatíoo..., parakaló
Could you put this in the safe, please?	Μπορώ να αφήσω αυτό στο χρηματοκιβώτιό σας;
	boró nafíso aftó sto chrimatokivótiósas?
Could you wake me at...tomorrow?	Μπορείτε να με ξυπνήσετε αύριο στις...;
	boríte na me xipnísete ávrio stis ...?
Could you find a babysitter for me?	Μπορείτε να μου βρείτε μια μπέιμπυ σίτερ;
	boríte na moo vríte mya béibi-síter?
Could I have an extra blanket?	Μπορώ να έχω κι άλλη μια κουβέρτα;
	boró na écho kyáli mía koovérta?
What days do the cleaners come in?	Ποιές μέρες καθαρίζουν τα δωμάτια;
	pyes méres katharízoon ta dhomátya?
When are the sheets/towels/dish towels changed?	Πότε αλλάζουν τα σεντόνια/τις πετσέτες/τις πετσέτες για τα πιάτα;
	póte alázoon ta sendónya/tis petsétes/tis petsétes ya ta pyáta?

🔔 .4 Complaints

We can't sleep because of the noise	Δεν μπορούμε να κοιμηθούμε μ' αυτό το θόρυβο
	dhemboróome na kimithóome maftó to thórivo
Could you turn the radio down, please?	Μπορείτε να χαμηλώσετε λίγο το ραδιόφωνο;
	boríte na chamilósete lígho to radhiófono?
We're out of toilet paper	Τελείωσε το χαρτί υγείας
	telíose to chartí iyías
There aren't any.../there's not enough...	Δεν έχει/δεν έχει αρκετά...
	dhen éhi/dhen éhi arketá...
The bed linen's dirty	Τα κλινοσκεπάσματα είναι βρώμικα
	ta klinoskepázmata íne vromiká
The room hasn't been cleaned	Δεν καθάρισαν το δωμάτιο
	dhen kathárisan to dhomátyo

The kitchen is not clean___ Η κουζίνα δεν είναι καθαρή
i koozína dhen íne katharí

The kitchen utensils are___ Τα κουζινικά είναι βρώμικα
dirty *ta kooziniká íne vrómika*

The heater's not___ Το καλοριφέρ δε λειτουργεί
working *to kalorifér dhe litooryí*

There's no (hot) ___ Δεν έχει (ζεστό) νερό/ρεύμα
water/electricity *dhen éhi (zestó) neró/révma*

...is broken___ ...χάλασε
...chálase

Could you have that___ Μπορείτε να το διορθώσετε;
seen to? *boríte na to dhiorthósete?*

Could I have another ___ Μπορείτε να μου δώσετε ένα άλλο
room? δωμάτιο
boríte na moo dhósete éna álo dhomátyo

The bed creaks terribly ___ Το κρεβάτι τρίζει φοβερά
to kreváti trízi foverá

The bed sags terribly ___ Το κρεβάτι βουλιάζει φοβερά
to kreváti voolyázi foverá

There's a lot of noise ___ Έχει πάρα πολύ θόρυβο
éhi pára polí thórivo

There are bugs/insects___ Έχουμε πολλά ζωύφια/έντομα
in our room *échoome polá zoífya/éndoma*

This place is full___ Είναι γεμάτο κουνούπια εδώ
of mosquitos *íne yemáto koonóopya edhó*

– cockroaches___ Είναι γεμάτο κατσαρίδες εδώ
íne yemáto katsarídhes edhó

7 .5 Departure

See also 8.2 Settling the bill

I'm leaving tomorrow. ___ Αύριο φεύγω. Μπορώ να πληρώσω τώρα;
Could I pay my bill, please? *ávrio févgho. boró na pliróso tóra?*

What time should we ___ Τί ώρα πρέπει να φύγουμε από...;
check out? *ti óra prépi na fíghoome apó...?*

Could I have my deposit/ ___ Μου δίνετε πίσω την εγγύηση/το διαβατήριό μου;
passport back, please? *moo dhínete píso tin engíisi/to dhiavatíriómoo?*

We're in a terrible hurry ___ Βιαζόμαστε πολύ
vyazómaste polí

Could you forward ___ Μπορείτε να στείλετε τα γράμματά μου σ'
my mail to this address? αυτή τη διεύθυνση;
boríte na stílete ta ghrámatámoo saftí ti dhiéfthinsi?

Could we leave our___ Μπορούμε να αφήσουμε τις βαλίτσες μας
luggage here until we εδώ μέχρι να φύγουμε;
leave? *boróome nafísoome tis valítses mas edhó méchri na fíghoome?*

Thanks for your ___ Ευχαριστώ για τη φιλοξενία σας
hospitality *efcharistó ya ti filoxeníasas*

Money matters

Money matters

Money matters

● **In general,** banks are open to the public between 8am and 2pm; they are closed on Saturdays. Exchange bureaus are open until 10pm. Money and travelers checks can also be changed in most of the larger hotels. In the islands the post offices often have currency changing facilities. To exchange currency a proof of identity is usually required. The sign *ΣΥΝΑΛΛΑΓΜΑ* indicates that money can be exchanged.

8.1 **B**anks

Where can I find a_____ bank/an exchange office around here?	Υπάρχει εδώ κοντά καμιά τράπεζα/κανένα γραφείο συναλλάγματος; *ipárchi edhó kondá kamyá trápeza/kanéna ghrafío sinalághmatos?*
Where can I cash this_____ traveler's check/giro check?	Πού μπορώ να εξαργυρώσω αυτή την ταξιδιωτική επιταγή/ταχυδρομική επιταγή; *poo boró na exaryiróso aftí tin taxidhiotikí epitayí/ tachidhromikí epitayí?*
Can I cash this...here? _____	Μπορώ εδώ να εξαργυρώσω αυτό το...; *boró edhó na exaryiróso avtó to...?*
Can I withdraw money_____ on my credit card here?	Μπορώ να πάρω λεφτά εδώ με μια πιστωτική κάρτα; *boró na páro leftá edhó me mya pistotikí kárta?*
What's the minimum/_____ maximum amount?	Ποιό είναι το ελάχιστο ποσό/το ανώτατο ποσό; *pyo íne to eláchisto posó/to anótato posó?*
Can I take out less_____ than that?	Μπορώ να πάρω και μικρότερο ποσό; *boró na páro ke mikrótero posó?*
I've had some money_____ transferred here. Has it arrived yet?	Έκανα ένα τηλεγραφικό έμβασμα. Έφτασε το έμβασμα; *ékana éna tileghrafikó émvazma. éftase to émvazma?*
These are the details _____ of my bank in the US	Αυτά είναι τα στοιχεία της τράπεζάς μου στης Ηνωμενες Πολιτειες *aftá íne ta stihía tis trápezásmoo stis enoménes poleties*
This is my bank/giro_____ number	Αυτός είναι ο αριθμός λογαριασμού μου *aftós íne o arithmós loghariazmóomoo*
I'd like to change _____ some money	Θα ήθελα ν' αλλάξω χρήματα *tha íthela naláxo chrímata*
– pounds into... _____	λίρες στερλίνες για... *líres sterlínes ya...*
– dollars into... _____	δολλάρια για... *dholária ya...*
What's the exchange _____ rate?	Ποιά είναι η ισοτιμία; *pya íne i isotimía?*
Could you give me _____ some small change with it?	Μπορείτε να μου δώσετε και λίγα ψιλά, παρακαλώ; *boríte na moo dhósete ke lígha psilá, parakaló;*
This is not right _____	Αυτό είναι λάθος *avtó íne láthos*

Υπογράψετε εδώ_____	Sign here, please.
Συμπληρώσετε αυτό το χαρτί_____	Fill this out, please.
Μπορώ να δω το διαβατήριό σας; _____	Could I see your passport, please?
Μπορώ να δω την ταυτότητα σας; _____	Could I see some identification, please?
Μπορώ να δω την ταχυδρομική _____ σας κάρτα;	Could I see your girobank card, please?
Μπορώ να δω την τραπεζική _____ σας κάρτα;	Could I see your bank card, please?

 .2 Settling the bill

Could you put it on_____ my bill?	Μπορείτε να το γράψετε στο λογαριασμό μου; _boríte na to ghrápsete sto loghariazmómoo?_
Does this amount _____ include the tip?	(Στο ποσό αυτό) συμπεριλαμβάνεται η εξυπηρέτηση; _(sto posó aftó) simberilamvánete i exipirétisi?_
Can I pay by...?_____	Μπορώ να πληρώσω με...; _boró na pliróso me...?_
Can I pay by credit card?___	Μπορώ να πληρώσω με πιστωτική κάρτα; _boró na pliróso me pistotikí kárta?_
Can I pay by traveler's _____ check?	Μπορώ να πληρώσω με ταξιδιωτική επιταγή; _boró na pliróso me taxidhyotikí epitayí?_
Can I pay with foreign _____ currency?	Μπορώ να πληρώσω με ξένο συνάλλαγμα; _boró na pliróso me xéno sinálaghma?_
You've given me too _____ much/you haven't given me enough change	Μου δώσατε πίσω πάρα πολλά/πολύ λίγα _moo dhósate píso pára polá/polí lígha_

Δε δεχόμαστε πιστωτικές _____ κάρτες/ταξιδιωτικές επιταγές/ξένο συνάλλαγμα	We don't accept credit cards/traveler's checks/foreign currency

Could you check this _____ again, please?	Μπορείτε να το ξαναελέγξετε, παρακαλώ; _boríte na to xanaelénxete, parakaló?_
Could I have a receipt, _____ please?	Μπορώ να έχω μια απόδειξη/το λογαριασμό; _boró na écho mya apódhixi/to loghariazmó?_
I don't have enough _____ money on me	Δεν έχω αρκετά χρήματα επάνω μου _dhen écho arketá chrímata epánomoo_
This is for you _____	ορίστε, αυτό είναι για σας _oríste, aftó íne ya sas_
Keep the change _____	Κρατήστε τα ρέστα _kratíste ta résta_

Money matters

8

Mail and telephone

Mail and telephone

For giros, see 8 Money matters

● **In large towns** post offices are open from Monday to Friday between 7.30am and 8pm; in many such towns they are also open on Saturdays. In smaller towns the opening times are variable. Greek post offices can be recognized by the sign ΕΛΤΑ. Giro cards can be used there.

Stamps (γραμματόσημα) are also available in kiosks (περίπτερα) and in tourist areas they are often also sold in small souvenir and postcard shops.

γραμματόσημα	ταχυδρομικές επιταγές	τηλεγραφήματα
stamps	money orders	telegrams
δέματα		
packages		

Where's...?	Πού είναι...;
	poo íne...?
Where's the post office?	Υπάρχει εδώ κοντά κανένα ταχυδρομείο;
	ipárchi edhó kondá kanéna tahidhromío?
Where's the main post office?	Πού είναι το κεντρικό ταχυδρομείο;
	poo íne to kendtrikó tahidhromío?
Where's the mailbox?	Υπάρχει εδώ κοντά ένα γραμματοκιβώτιο;
	ipárchi edhó kondá éna ghramatokivótyo?
Which counter should I go to...?	Σε ποιά θυρίδα πρέπει να πάω για...;
	se pya thirídha prépi na páo ya...?
– to send a fax	Σε ποιά θυρίδα πρέπει να πάω για να στείλω ένα φαξ;
	se pya thirídha prépi na páo ya na stílo éna fax?
– to change money	Σε ποιά θυρίδα πρέπει να πάω για να αλλάξω χρήματα;
	se pya thirídha prépi na páo ya naláxo chrímata?
– to change giro checks	Σε ποιά θυρίδα πρέπει να πάω για να εξαργυρώσω τα ταχυδρομικά τσεκ;
	se pya thirídha prépi na páo ya na exaryiróso ta tahidhromiká tsek?
– for a Telegraph Money Order?	Σε ποιά θυρίδα πρέπει να πάω για τηλεγραφικό έμβασμα;
	se pya thirídha prépi na páo ya tileghrafikó émvazma?
General delivery	Ποστ-ρεστάντ
	post-restánt
Is there any mail for me? My name's...	Έχετε γράμματα για μένα; Το όνομά μου είναι...
	éhete ghrámata ya ména? to ónomámoo íne...

Mail and telephone

Stamps

What's the postage _____ for a...to...?	Τι γραμματόσημα χρειάζομαι για...; *ti ghramatósima chriázome ya...?*
Are there enough _____ stamps on it?	Φτάνουν αυτά τα γραμματόσημα; *ftánoon aftá ta ghramatósima*
I'd like... ...drachma_____ stamps	Θα ήθελα...γραμματόσημα των... *tha íthela...ghramatósima ton...*
I'd like to send this... _____	Θέλω να το στείλω αυτό ... *thélo na to stílo aftó...*
– express _____	Θέλω να το στείλω αυτό επείγον *thélo na to stílo aftó epíghon*
– by air mail _____	Θέλω να το στείλω αυτό αεροπορικώς *thélo na to stílo aftó aeroporikós*
– by registered mail _____	Θέλω να το στείλω αυτό συστημένο *thélo na to stílo aftó sistiméno*

Telegram / fax

I'd like to send a _____ telegram to...	Θα ήθελα να στείλω ένα τηλεγράφημα σε... *tha íthela na stílo éna tileghráfima se...*
How much is that _____ per word?	Πόσο κάνει η λέξη; *póso káni i léxi?*
This is the text I want_____ to send	Αυτό είναι το κείμενο που θέλω να στείλω *aftó íne to kímeno poo thélo na stílo*
Shall I fill out the form_____ myself?	Να συμπληρώσω μόνος/μόνη μου το έντυπο; *na simplíroso mónos/móni moo to éndipo?*
Can I make photocopies/___ send a fax here?	Μπορώ να κάνω φωτοτυπίες/να στείλω ένα φαξ; *boró edhó na káno fototipíes/na stílo éna fax?*
How much is it_____ per page?	Πόσο κάνει η σελίδα; *póso káni i selídha?*

9.2 Telephone

See also 1.8 Telephone alphabet

● **In Greece** you cannot make phone calls from an ordinary post office. The special telephone offices are marked OTE. Here you make the call and then pay. In tourist resorts there are also usually a number of public phone booths (for which a phone card is advisable) from which you can make international calls, and local calls can be made from kiosks.
When phoning someone in Greece, you will not be greeted with the subscriber's name or number, but simply with *εμπρός* or *ορίστε*.

Is there a phone booth _____ around here?	Υπάρχει εδώ κοντά κανένας τηλεφωνικός θάλαμος; *ipárchi edhó kondá kanénas tilefonikós thálamos?*
Could I use your _____ phone, please?	Μπορώ να χρησιμοποιήσω το τηλέφωνό σας; *boró na chrisimopiíso to tiléfonósas?*
Do you have a _____ (city/region)...phone directory?	Εχετε ένα τηλεφωνικό κατάλογο της πόλης.../της περιοχής...; *éhete éna tilefonikó katálogho tis pólis/tis periohís...?*
Could you give me...? _____	Μπορείτε να μου δώσετε...; *boríte na moo dhósete...?*

– the number for _____ international directory assistance	Μπορείτε να μου δώσετε τον αριθμό για τις πληροφορίες εξωτερικού; *boríte na moo dhósete ton airithmó ya tis pliroforíes exoterikóo?*
– the number of room... ___	Μπορείτε να μου δώσετε τον αριθμό του δωματίου; *boríte na moo dhósete ton arithmó too dhomatíoo...?*
– the international _____ access code	Μπορείτε να μου δώσετε το διεθνή κωδικό της/του/των...; *boríte na moo dhósete to dhiethní kódhiko tis/too/ton...?*
– the country code for... ____	Μπορείτε να μου δώσετε τον κωδικό της...; *boríte na moo dhósete tongódhiko tis...?*
– the area code for... _____	Μπορείτε να μου δώσετε τον κωδικό της πόλης...; *boríte na moo dhósete tongódhiko tis pólis...?*
– the number of... _____	Μπορείτε να μου δώσετε τον αριθμό τηλεφώνου του/της...; *boríte na moo dhósete ton arithmó tilefónoo too/tis...?*
Could you check if this ____ number's correct?	Μπορείτε να ελέγξετε αν είναι σωστός αυτός ο αριθμός; *boríte na elénxete an íne sostós o arithmós?*
Can I dial international ____ direct?	Μπορώ να τηλεφωνήσω αυτόματα στο εξωτερικό; *boró na tilefoníso aftómata sto exoterikó?*
Do I have to go through ___ the switchboard?	Πρέπει να τηλεφωνήσω μέσω της τηλεφωνήτριας; *prépi na tilefoníso méso tis tilefonítrias?*
Do I have to dial '0' first? __	Πρέπει να πάρω πρώτα το μηδέν; *prépi na páro próta to midhén?*
Do I have to reserve _____ my calls?	Πρέπει να ζητήσω μια συνδιάλεξη; *prépi na zitíso mya sindhiálexi?*
Could you dial this _____ number for me, please?	Μπορείτε να μου πάρετε τον εξής αριθμό, παρακαλώ; *boríte na moo párete ton exís arithmó, parakaló?*
Could you put me _____ through to.../extension..., please?	Μπορείτε να με συνδέσετε με.../με το εσωτερικό τηλέφωνο...; *boríte na me sindhésete me.../me to esoterikó tiléfono...?*
I'd like to place a _____ collect call to...	Θέλω να τηλεφωνήσω με έξοδα του δέκτη... *thélo na thlefoníso me éxodha too dhékti...*
What's the charge per ____ minute?	Πόσο κάνει το λεπτό; *póso káni to leptó?*
Have there been any _____ calls for me?	Μου τηλεφώνησε κανείς; *moo tilefónise kanís?*

The conversation

Who is this, please? _____	Ποιός είναι; *pyos íne?*
Hello, this is... _____	Γειά σας, είμαι ο/η... *Yásas, íme o/i...*

Is this...? _____	Εσείς είστε ο/η...;
	esís íste o/i ...?
I'm sorry, I've dialed_____	Συγγνώμη, πήρα λάθος αριθμό
the wrong number	*sighnómi, píra láthos arithmó*
I can't hear you _____	Δε σας ακούω καλά
	dhe sas akóo-o kalá
I'd like to speak to... _____	Θα ήθελα να μιλήσω με το (ν)/τη (ν)...
	tha íthela na milíso me to(n)/ti(n)...
Is there anybody _____	Ξέρει κανείς αγγλικά;
who speaks English?	*xéri kanís anglıká?*
Extension..., please_____	Μπορείτε να με συνδέσετε με το εσωτερικό
	τηλέφωνο...;
	boríte na me sindhésete me to esoterikó
	tiléfono...?
Could you ask him/her_____	Του/της λέτε να με πάρει τηλέφωνο;
to call me back?	*too/tis léte na me pári tiléfono?*
My name's... _____	Το όνομα μου είναι...Ο αριθμός τηλεφώνου
My number's...	είναι...
	to ónomámoo íne...o arithmós tilefónoo íne...
Could you tell him/her _____	Θέλετε να πείτε ότι τηλεφώνησα;
I called?	*thélete na píte óti tilefónisa?*
I'll call back tomorrow _____	Θα του/της ξανατηλεφωνήσω αύριο
	tha too/tis xanatilefoníso ávrio

Σας ζητούν στο τηλέφωνο _____	There's a phone call for you
Πρέπει να πάρετε πρώτα το μηδέν_____	You have to dial '0' first
'Ένα λεπτό, παρακαλώ _____	One moment, please
Δεν απαντά _____	There's no answer
Η γραμμή είναι κατειλημμένη_____	The line's busy
Περιμένετε λιγάκι;_____	Do you want to hold?
Σας συνδέω τώρα _____	Connecting you
Πήρατε λάθος αριθμό _____	You've got a wrong number
Αυτή τη στιγμή λείπει ο/η... _____	He's/she's not here right now
Μπορείτε να του τηλεφωνήσετε... _____	He'll/she'll be back...
Αυτός είναι ο αυτόματος τηλεφωνητής __	This is the answering
του/της...	machine of...

Shopping

10 **S**hopping

● **Opening times:** in general shops are open on Mondays, Wednesdays and Saturdays from 8am until 2.30pm and on Tuesdays, Thursdays and Fridays from 8am to 1pm and from 5pm to 8pm. In tourist areas in the summer, however, most shops open every evening and stay open until late. In the big cities opening hours vary, and many shops remain open throughout the day.

αγορά market	κατάστημα αθλητικών ειδών sports shop	περίπτερο kiosk
ανθοπωλείο florist	κατάστημα παιχνιδιών toy shop	πλυντήριο laundry
αρτοπωλείο (φούρνος) bakery	κατάστημα σουβενίρ souvenir shop	πολυκατάστημα department store
βιβλιοπωλείο bookshop	κοινόχρηστο πλυντήριο launderette	πρακτορείο ταξιδιών travel agency
γαλακτοπωλείο dairy product shop	κομμωτήριο ladies' hairdresser	ραφείο tailor
γουναράδικο furrier	κοσμηματοπωλείο jeweler	σούπερ-μάρκετ supermarket
ζαχαροπλαστείο confectioner (also acts as a café for its products)	κουρείο barber shop	στεγνοκαθαριστήριο dry cleaner
ινστιτούτο καλλονής beauty salon	κρεοπωλείο butcher	τσαγκάρης cobbler
ιχθυοπωλείο (ψαράδικο) fishmonger	μανάβικο greengrocer	υποδηματοπωλείο (παπουτσάδικο) shoe shop
καθαριστήριο cleaner	μοδίστρια dressmaker	φαρμακείο pharmacy
καπελάδικο hat shop	οπτικός optician	φωτογραφείο photographer/ camera shop
καπνοπωλείο tobacco shop	παλαιοπωλείο antique shop	χαρτοπωλείο stationer
	παντοπωλείο general store	ψιλικατζίδικο haberdasher

10 .1 **S**hopping conversations

Where can I get...? _____	Σε ποιό κατάστημα μπορώ να βρω...; *se pyo katástima boró na vro...?*
When does this shop _____ open?	Τί ώρα ανοίγει αυτό το μαγαζί; *ti óra aníyi aftó to maghazí?*
Could you tell me _____ where the...department is?	Μπορείτε να μου πείτε πού είναι το τμήμα...; *boríte na moo píte poo íne to tmíma...?*
Could you help me, _____ please? I'm looking for...	Μπορείτε να με βοηθήσετε; Ψάχνω... *boríte na me voithísete? Psáchno...*
Do you sell English/ _____ American newspapers?	Πουλάτε αγγλικές/αμερικανικές εφημερίδες; *pooláte anglikés/amerikanikés efimerídhes?*

Σας εξυπηρετεί κανείς; _____ **Are you being served?**

No, I'd like... _____ Όχι. Θα ήθελα...
 óhi. tha íthela...
I'm just looking, _____ Θα ρίξω μια ματιά, αν επιτρέπεται
 if that's all right *tha ríxo mya matyá, an epitrépete*

Τίποτ' άλλο; _____ **Anything else?**

Yes, I'd also like... _____ Ναι, θέλω και...
 ne, thélo ke...
No, thank you. That's all ___ Όχι, ευχαριστώ. Τίποτ' άλλο
 óhi, efcharistó. típotálo
Could you show me...? ____ Μπορείτε να μου δείξετε...
 boríte na moo díxete
I'd prefer... _____ Προτιμώ...
 protimó...
This is not what I'm _____ Δεν είναι αυτό που ψάχνω
 looking for *dhen íne aftó poo psáchno*
Thank you. I'll keep_____ Ευχαριστώ. Θα κοιτάξω και αλλού
 looking *efcharistó. tha kitáxo ke alóo*
Do you have _____ Μήπως έχετε κάτι που είναι...
 something...? *mípos éhete káti poo íne...*
– less expensive?_____ Μήπως έχετε κάτι πιο φτηνό;
 mípos éhete káti pyo ftinó?
– something smaller?_____ Μήπως έχετε κάτι πιο μικρό;
 mípos éhete káti pyo mikró?
– something larger? _____ Μήπως έχετε κάτι πιο μεγάλο;
 mípos éhete káti pyo meghálo?
I'll take this one _____ Θα πάρω αυτό
 tha páro aftó
Does it come with _____ Έχει οδηγίες χρήσεως μέσα;
 instructions? *éhi odhiyíes chríseos mésa?*
It's too expensive _____ Είναι πολύ ακριβό
 íne polí akrivó
I'll give you... _____ Θα σας δώσω...
 tha sas dhóso...
Could you keep this for ____ Μπορείτε να φυλάξετε αυτό για μένα; Θα
 me? I'll come back for it περάσω σε λίγο να το πάρω
 later *boríte na filáxete aftó ya ména? tha peráso*
 se lígho na to páro
Have you got a bag _____ Μου δίνετε μία σακούλα, παρακαλώ;
 for me, please? *moo dhínete mya sakóola, parakaló?*
Could you giftwrap_____ Μπορείτε να το τυλίξετε για δώρο,
 it, please? παρακαλώ;
 boríte na to tilíxete ya dhóro, parakaló?

Shopping

10

Λυπάμαι, δεν το έχουμε _____	I'm sorry, we don't have that
Λυπάμαι, μας έχει εξαντληθεί _____	I'm sorry, we're sold out
Λυπάμαι, θα το έχουμε πάλι... _____	I'm sorry, that won't be in until...
Μπορείτε να πληρώσετε στο ταμείο _____	You can pay at the cash desk
Δε δεχόμαστε πιστωτικές κάρτες _____	We don't accept credit cards
Δε δεχόμαστε ταξιδιωτικές επιταγές_____	We don't accept traveler's checks
Δε δεχόμαστε ξένο συνάλλαγμα_____	We don't accept foreign currency

10.2 Food

I'd like a hundred _____ grams of..., please	Θα ήθελα εκατό γραμμάρια ... *ha íthela ekató ghramárya...*
– half a kilo of... _____	Θα ήθελα μισό κιλό... *tha íthela misó kiló...*
– a kilo of... _____	Θα ήθελα ένα κιλό *tha íthela éna kiló...*
Could you...it for me, _____ please?	Μπορείτε να μου το...: *boríte na moo to...*
Could you slice it/ _____ chop it for me, please?	Μπορείτε να μου το κόψετε σε φέτες/σε κομμάτια; *boríte na moo to kópsete se fétes/se komátya?*
Could you grate it _____ for me, please?	Μπορείτε να μου το τρίψετε; *boríte na moo to trípsete?*
Can I order it?_____	Μπορώ να το παραγγείλω; *boró na to paranghílo?*
I'll pick it up tomorrow/ ____ at...	Θα περάσω αύριο/στις...να το πάρω *tha peráso ávrio/stis...na to páro*
Can you eat/drink this? ____	Αυτό τρώγεται/πίνεται; *aftó tróyete/pínete?*
What's in it? _____	Τί έχει μέσα; *ti éhi mésa?*

10.3 Clothing and shoes

I saw something in the ____ window. Shall I point it out?	Είδα κάτι στη βιτρίνα. Να σας το δείξω; *ídha káti sti vitrína. na sas to dhíxo?*
I'd like something to_____ go with this	Θέλω κάτι που να ταιριάζει μ' αυτό *thélo káti poo na teryázi maftó*
Do you have shoes _____ to match this?	Εχετε ασσορτί παπούτσια; *éhete asortí papóotsya?*
I'm a size...in the US_____	Στης Ηνωμενες Πολιτειες φοράω νούμερο... *stis enoménes poletíes foráo nóomero...*
Can I try this on? _____	Μπορώ να το δοκιμάσω; *boró na to dhokimáso?*
Where's the fitting room? __	Πού είναι το δοκιμαστήριο; *poo íne to dhokimastírio*

Shopping

It doesn't fit _____	Δε μου κάνει
	dhe moo káni
This is the right size _____	Αυτό είναι το σωστό νούμερο
	aftó íne to sostó nóomero
It doesn't suit me _____	Δε μου πάει
	dhe moo pái
Do you have this/ _____ these in...?	Το έχετε και σε...;
	to éhete ke se...?
The heel's too high/low _____	Το τακούνι είναι πολύ ψηλό/χαμηλό
	to takóoni íne polí psiló/chamiló
Is this/are these _____ genuine leather?	Είναι αυτό/αυτά από γνήσιο δέρμα;
	íne aftó/aftá apó ghnísyo dhérma?
I'm looking for a... _____ for a...-year-old baby/child	Ψάχνω ένα...για ένα μωρό/παιδί...χρονών
	psáchno éna...ya éna moró/pedhí...chronón
I'd like a...(made of)... _____	Θα ήθελα ένα...από...
	tha íthela éna...apó...
– silk _____	Θα ήθελα ένα...από μετάξι
	tha íthela éna...apó metáxi
– cotton _____	Θα ήθελα ένα...από βαμβάκι
	tha íthela éna...apó vamváki
– woolen _____	Θα ήθελα ένα...από μαλλί
	tha íthela éna...apó malí
– linen _____	Θα ήθελα ένα...από λινό
	tha íthela éna...apó linó
What temperature _____ can I wash it at?	Σε ποιά θερμοκρασία μπορώ να το πλύνω;
	se pya thermokrasía boró na to plíno?
Will it shrink in the _____ wash?	Δε μαζεύει;
	dhe mazévi?

Καθαριστήριο	Με το χέρι	Μην το στεγνώνετε
dry clean	**by hand**	στο στεγνωτήριο
Κρεμάστε το	Μη	**do not tumble dry**
υγρό	σιδερώνετε	Στο πλυντήριο
do not spin dry	**do not iron**	**machine wash**

At the cobbler

Could you mend _____ these shoes?	Μπορείτε να φτιάξετε αυτά τα παπούτσια;
	boríte na ftyáxete aftá ta papóotsya?
Could you put new _____ soles/heels on these?	Μπορείτε να βάλετε καινούριες
	σόλες/καινούρια τακούνια σ΄ αυτά;
	boríte na válete kenóoryes sóles/kenóorya
	takóonya saftá?
When will they be _____ ready?	πότε θα είναι έτοιμα;
	póte tha íne étima?
I'd like... _____	Θα ήθελα...
	tha íthela...
– a can of shoe polish _____	Θα ήθελα ένα κουτάκι βερνίκι
	tha íthela éna kootáki verníki papootsyón
– a pair of shoelaces _____	Θα ήθελα ένα ζευγάρι κορδόνια
	tha íthela éna zevghári kordhónya

I'd like a film for this_____ camera, please	Θα ήθελα ένα φιλμ για αυτή τη μηχανή
	ha ithela éna film ya avtí ti mihaní
– a one twenty-six_____ cartridge	Θα ήθελα μια κασέτα των 126
	tha íthela mya kaséta ton ekató íkosi éxI
– a slide film_____	Θα ήθελα ένα φιλμ για σλάιτς
	tha íthela éna film ya slaidz
– a film cartridge _____	Θα ήθελα μια κασέτα φιλμ
	tha íthela mya kaséta film
– a videotape _____	Θα ήθελα μια βιντεοταινία
	tha íthela mya videotenía
color/black and white_____	έγχρωμο/ασπρόμαυρο
	énchromo/asprómavro
super eight _____	σούπερ οχτώ
	sóoper ochtó
12/24/36 exposures_____	δωδεκάρι/εικοσιτεσσάρι/τριανταεξάρι
	dhodekári/ikositesári/triandaexári
ASA/DIN number_____	αριθμό ΑΣΑ
	arithmó asa
daylight film _____	φιλμ για κανονικό φως
	film ya kanonikó fos
film for artificial light _____	φιλμ για τεχνητό φως
	film ya technitó fos

Problems

Could you load the _____ film for me, please?	Μπορείτε να βάλετε το φιλμ στη μηχανή, παρακαλώ;
	boríte na válete to film sti michaní, parakaló
Could you take the film ____ out for me, please?	Μπορείτε να βγάλετε το φιλμ από τη μηχανή, παρακαλώ;
	boríte na vghálete to film apó ti michaní, parakaló
Should I replace_____ the batteries?	Πρέπει ν' αλλάξω τις μπαταρίες;
	prépi naláxo tis bataríes?
Could you have a look_____ at my camera, please? It's not working	Μπορείτε να κοιτάξετε τη μηχανή μου; Δε λειτουργεί
	boríte na kitáxete ti michanímou? dhe litooryí
The...is broken _____	Το...είναι χαλασμένο
	to...íne chalazméno
The film's jammed _____	Το φιλμ έχει μπλεχτεί
	to film éhi blechtí
The film's broken_____	Το φιλμ κόπηκε
	to film kópike
The flash isn't working ____	Το φλας δε λειτουργεί
	to flash dhe litooryí

Processing and prints

I'd like to have this film ____ developed/printed, please	Θα ήθελα να εμφανίσετε/εκτυπώσετε αυτό το φιλμ
	tha íthela na emfanísete/ektipósete aftó to film
I'd like...prints from_____ each negative	Θα ήθελα...φωτογραφίες από κάθε αρνητικό
	tha íthela...fotographíes apó káthe arnitikó
glossy/matte _____	γυαλιστερό/ματ
	yalisteró/mat

6x9 _____	έξι επί εννιά
	éxi epí enyá
I'd like to reorder _____	Θέλω να παραγγείλω κι άλλες
these photos	φωτογραφίες απ' αυτές
	thélo na parangilo kyáles fotoghrafíes apaftés
I'd like to have this _____	Θα ήθελα να μου μεγεθύνετε αυτή τη
photo enlarged	φωτογραφία
	tha íthela na moo meyethínete aftí ti fotoghrafía
How much is_____	Πόσο κάνει η εμφάνιση;
processing?	*póso káni i emfánisi?*
– printing _____	Πόσο κάνει η εκτύπωση;
	póso káni i ektíposi?
– it to reorder _____	Πόσο κάνει η παραγγελία έξτρα
	φωτογραφιών;
	póso káni i paranghelía éxtra fotoghrafyón?
– the enlargement _____	Πόσο κάνει η μεγέθυνση;
	póso káni i meyénthisi?
When will they _____	Πότε θα είναι έτοιμες;
be ready?	*póte tha íne étimes?*

10.5 At the hairdresser's

Do I have to make an _____	Πρέπει να κλείσω ραντεβού;
appointment?	*prépi na klíso randevó?*
Can I come in right _____	Μπορείτε να με εξυπηρετήσετε αμέσως;
now?	*boríte na me exipiritísete amésos?*
How long will I have_____	Πόση ώρα πρέπει να περιμένω;
to wait?	*pósi óra prépi na periméno?*
I'd like a shampoo/ _____	Θα ήθελα να λούσετε/κόψετε τα μαλλιά
haircut	μου
	tha íthela na lóosete/kópsete ta malyámoo
I'd like a shampoo for _____	Θα ήθελα ένα σαμπουάν για λιπαρά/ξηρά
oily/dry hair, please	μαλλιά
	tha íthela éna sampwán ya lipará/xirá malyá
an anti-dandruff_____	Θα ήθελα ένα σαμπουάν κατά της
shampoo	πιτυρίδας;
	tha íthela éna sampwán katá tis pitirídhas
– a shampoo for_____	Θα ήθελα ένα σαμπουάν για μαλλιά με
permed/colored hair	περμανάντ/για βαμμένα μαλλιά
	tha íthela éna sampwán ya malyá me permanánt/ya vaména malyá
– a color rinse shampoo ___	Θα ήθελα ένα σαμπουάν με χρώμα
	tha íthela éna sampwán me chróma
– a shampoo with _____	Θα ήθελα ένα σαμπουάν με κρέμα
conditioner	λουσίματος
	tha íthela éna sampwán me kréma loosímatos
– highlights _____	Θα ήθελα ένα κουπ-σολέι
	tha íthela éna koop-soléi
Do you have a color _____	Έχετε ένα δειγματολόγιο χρωμάτων;
chart, please?	*éhete éna dighmatolóyio chromáton?*
I want to keep it the _____	Θέλω να κρατήσω το ίδιο χρώμα
same color	*thélo na kratíso to ídhyo chróma*
I'd like it darker/lighter _____	Τα θέλω πιο σκούρα/πιο ανοιχτά
	ta thélo pyo skóora/pyo anichtá

Shopping

I'd like short bangs _____ Θέλω τη φράντζα μου πιο κοντή
thélo ti frándza moo pyo kondí

Not too short at the back __ Θέλω να μην είναι πολύ κοντά πίσω
thélo na min íne polí kondá píso

Not too long here _____ Θέλω να μην είναι πολύ μακριά εδώ
thélo na min íne polí makriá edhó

I'd like/I don't want _____ (Δε) θέλω να έχω (πολλές) μπούκλες
(many) curls *(dhe) thélo na écho (polés) bóokles*

It needs a little/_____ Τα θέλω λίγο πιο κοντά/πολύ πιο κοντά
a lot taken off *ta thélo lígho pyo kondá /polí pyo kondá*

I want a completely _____ Θέλω τελείως διαφορετικό στυλ
different style *thélo telíos dhiaforetikó stil*

I'd like it the same... _____ Θέλω τα μαλλιά μου σαν...
thélo ta malyámoo san...

– as that lady's _____ Θέλω τα μαλλιά μου σαν αυτής της κυρίας
thélo ta malyámoo san aftís tis kirías

– as in this photo_____ Θέλω τα μαλλιά μου όπως σ' αυτή τη
φωτογραφία
thélo ta malyámoo ópos saftí ti fotoghrafía

Could you put the _____ Μπορείτε να βάλετε την κάσκα πιο
drier up/down a bit? ψηλά/πιο χαμηλά;
boríte na válete tingáska pyo psilá/pyo chamilá?

I'd like a facial_____ Θα ήθελα μια μάσκα προσώπου
tha íthela mya máska prosópoo

– a manicure _____ Θα ήθελα ένα μανικιούρ
tha íthela éna manikyóor

– a massage _____ Θα ήθελα ένα μασάζ
tha íthela éna masáz

Could you trim my..., _____ Μπορείτε να κόψετε λίγο...μου, παρακαλώ;
please? *boríte na kópsete lígho...moo, parakaló?*

Could you trim_____ Μπορείτε να κόψετε λίγο τη φράντζα μου,
my bangs? παρακαλώ;
boríte na kópsete lígho ti frándzamoo, parakaló?

– my beard? _____ Μπορείτε να κόψετε λίγο τα γένια μου,
παρακαλώ;
boríte na kópsete lígho ta yényamoo, parakaló?

– my moustache? _____ Μπορείτε να κόψετε λίγο το μουστάκι μου,
παρακαλώ;
boríte na kópsete lígho to moostákimoo, parakaló?

I'd like a shave, please_____ Ξύρισμα, παρακαλώ
xírizma, parakaló

I'd like a wet shave, _____ Θέλω να με ξυρίσετε με ξυράφι, παρακαλώ
please *thélo na me xirísete me xiráfi, parakaló*

Shopping

10

Πώς θέλετε να κόψω τα μαλλιά σας;	How do you want it cut?
Πιο στυλ θέλετε;	What style did you have in mind?
Τί χρώμα θέλετε;	What color did you want it?
Είναι καλή αυτή η θερμοκρασία;	Is the temperature all right for you?
Θέλετε κάτι να διαβάσετε;	Would you like something to read?
Θέλετε να πιείτε κάτι;	Would you like a drink?
Σας αρέσει έτσι;	Is this what you had in mind?

At the Tourist Information Center

11 .1 **P**laces of interest

Where's the Tourist _____ Information Center, please?	Πού βρίσκεται το γραφείο τουρισμού; *poo vrískete to grhafío toorizmóo?*
Do you have a city map?___	Έχετε ένα χάρτη της πόλης; *éhete éna chárti tis pólis?*
Could you give me _____ some information about...?	Μπορείτε να μου δώσετε πληροφορίες για... *boríte na moo dhósete pliroforíes ya ...*
How much is that? _____	Πόσο σας οφείλουμε; *póso sas ofíloome?*
What are the main _____ places of interest?	Ποιά είναι τα σπουδαιότερα αξιοθέατα; *pya íne ta spoodheótera axiothéata?*
Could you point them _____ out on the map?	Μπορείτε να τα δείξετε στο χάρτη; *boríte na to dhíxete sto chárti?*
What do you _____ recommend?	Τί μας συμβουλεύετε; *ti mas simvoolévete?*
We'll be here for a_____ few hours	Θα μείνουμε εδώ λίγες ώρες *tha mínoome edhó líyes óres*
– a day _____	Θα μείνουμε εδώ μία μέρα *tha mínoome edhó mía méra*
– a week _____	Θα μείνουμε εδώ μία εβδομάδα *tha mínoome edhó mía evdhomádha*
We're interested in... _____	Ενδιαφερόμαστε για... *endhiaferómaste ya ...*
Is there a scenic walk_____ around the city?	Μπορούμε να κάνουμε μια βόλτα στην πόλη; *boróome na kánoome mya vólta stimbóli?*
How long does it take? ____	Πόσο κρατάει; *póso kratái?*
Where does it start/end? ___	Πού είναι η αφετηρία/το τέρμα; *poo íne i afetería/to térma?*
Are there any boat _____ cruises here?	Υπάρχουν εδώ εκδρομικά καραβάκια; *ipárchoon edhó ekdhromiká karavákya?*
Where can we board? _____	Πού μπορούμε να μπαρκάρουμε; *poo boróome na barkároome?*
Are there any bus tours?___	Γίνονται εκδρομές με πούλμαν; *yínonde ekdhromés me póolman?*
Where do we get on? _____	Πού πρέπει να ανεβούμε; *poo prépi na anevóome?*
Is there a guide who_____ speaks English?	Υπάρχει ένας ξεναγός με αγγλικά; *ipárchi énas xenaghós me angliká?*
What trips can we take ____ around the area?	Τί εκδρομές μπορεί να κάνει κανείς σ' αυτή την περιοχή; *ti ekdhromés borí na káni aftí timberiohí?*
Are there any _____ excursions?	Υπάρχουν οργανωμένες εκδρομές; *ipárchoon orghanoménes ekdhromés?*
Where do they go to? _____	Για πού; *ya poo?*
We'd like to go to..._____	Θέλουμε να πάμε σε... *théloome na pàme se ...*
How long is the trip? _____	Πόσο κρατάει αυτή η διαδρομή; *póso kratái aftí i dhiadromí?*

How long do we stay in...?	Πόση ώρα θα μείνουμε σε...; *pósi óra tha mínoome se ...?*
Are there any guided tours?	Γίνονται ξεναγήσεις εκεί; *yínonde xenayísis ekí?*
How much free time will we have there?	Πόση ώρα θα έχουμε στη διάθεσή μας εκεί; *pósi óra tha échoome sti dhiáthesímas ekí?*
We want to go hiking	Θέλουμε να κάνουμε πεζοπορία *théloome na kánoome pezoporía*
Can we hire a guide?	Μπορούμε να νοικιάσουμε έναν ξεναγό; *boróome na nikyásoome énan xenaghó?*
Can I reserve mountain huts?	Μπορώ να κλείσω ένα ορειβατικό καταφύγιο; *boró na klíso éna orivatikó katafíyo?*
What time does... open/close?	Τί ώρα ανοίγει/κλείνει το...; *to óra aníyi/klíni to...?*
What days is...open/closed?	Ποιές μέρες είναι ανοιχτό/κλειστό το...; *pyes méres íne anichtó/klistó to ...?*
What's the admission price?	Πόσο κοστίζει η είσοδος; *póso kostízi i ísodhos?*
Is there a group discount?	Κάνετε έκπτωση για γκρουπ; *kánete ékptosi ya groop?*
Is there a child discount?	Κάνετε έκπτωση για παιδιά; *kánete ékptosi ya pedhyá?*
Is there a discount for seniors?	Κάνετε έκπτωση για ηλικιωμένους; *kánete ékptosi ya ilikyoménoos?*
Can I take (flash) photos/can I film here?	Επιτρέπεται εδώ η φωτογράφηση (με φλας)/η κινηματογράφηση; *epitrépete edhó i fotoghráfisi (me flash)/i kinimatoghráfisi?*
Do you have any postcards of...?	Πουλάτε κάρτες με...; *pooláte kártes me ...?*
Do you have an English...?	Εχετε ένα ... στα αγγλικά; *éhete éna ... sta angliká?*
– an English catalogue?	Εχετε ένα κατάλογο στα αγγλικά; *éhete éna katálogho sta angliká?*
– an English program?	Εχετε ένα πρόγραμμα στα αγγλικά; *éhete éna prógrama sta angliká?*
– an English brochure?	Εχετε ένα φυλλάδιο στα αγγλικά; *éhete éna filádhio sta angliká?*

11 .2 Going out

● **In Greece, theaters** and cinemas are usually open-air in the summer. Theater performances usually start at 8.30pm in winter, but later in summer. Cinemas show films between approximately 1.30 and 11pm.

Do you have this week's/month's entertainment guide?	Εχετε το Αθηνόραμα αυτής της εβδομάδας/αυτού του μήνα; *éhete to athinórama aftís tis evdhomádhas/aftóo too mína?*
What's on tonight?	Τί μπορούμε να κάνουμε απόψε; *ti boróome na kánoome apópse?*
We want to go to...	Θέλουμε να πάμε σε... *théloome na páme se ...*

Which films are showing?	Ποιές ταινίες παίζονται τώρα;
	pyes teníes pézonde tóra?
What sort of film is that?	Τί είδος ταινία είναι αυτή;
	ti ídhos tenía íne aftí?
suitable for	για όλες τις ηλικίες
the whole family	ya óles tis ilikíes
not suitable for	άνω των 12/16 χρονών
children	áno ton dhódheka me dekaéxi chronón
original version	πρωτότυπη έκδοση
	protótipi ékdhosi
subtitled	με υπότιτλους
	me ipotítloos
dubbed	ντουμπλαρισμένη
	dooblarizméni
Is it a continuous	Είναι παράσταση χωρίς διάλειμμα;
showing?	íne parástasi chorís dhiálima?
What's on at...?	Τί παίζουν στο...
	ti pézoon sto...
– the theater?	Τί παίζουν στο θέατρο;
	ti pézoon sto théatro?
– the concert hall?	Τί παίζουν στην αίθουσα συναυλιών;
	ti pézoon stin éthoosa sinavlyón?
– the opera?	Τί παίζουν στην όπερα;
	ti pézoon stin ópera?
Where can I find a good	Έχει εδώ κοντά καμμιά καλή ντίσκο;
disco around here?	éhi edhó kondá kamyá kalí dísko?
Is it members only?	Πρέπει να είσαι μέλος;
	prépi na íse mélos?
Where can I find a good	Έχει εδώ κοντά κανένα καλό νυχτερινό
nightclub around here?	κέντρο;
	éhi edhó kondá kanéna kaló nichterinó
	kéndro?
Is it evening wear only?	Είναι υποχρεωτική η βραδινή ενδυμασία;
	íne ipochreotikí i vradhiní endhimasía?
Should I/we wear	Ενδείκνυται η βραδινή ενδυμασία;
formal dress?	endhikníete i vradhiní endhimasía?
What time does the	Τί ώρα αρχίζει η παράσταση;
show start?	ti óra archízi i parástasi?
When's the next soccer	Πότε θα γίνει ο επόμενος ποδοσφαιρικός
match?	αγώνας;
	póte tha yíni o epómenos podhosferikós
	aghónas?
Who's playing?	Ποιές ομάδες παίζουν;
	pyes omádhes pézoon?
I'd like an escort for	Θέλω για απόψε ένα/μία έσκορτ. Μπορείτε
tonight. Could you arrange	να μου το κανονίσετε;
that for me?	thélo ya apópse éna/mía éskort. boríte na
	moo to kanonísete?

11 .3 **R**eserving tickets

Could you reserve some ___ tickets for us?	Μπορείτε να μας κλείσετε εισιτήρια; *boríte na mas klísete isitírya?*
We'd like to reserve..._____ seats/a table...	Θέλουμε...θέσεις/ένα τραπέζι *théloome...thésis/éna trapézi*
– in the orchestra_____	Θέλουμε...θέσεις στην πλατεία *théloome...thésis stimblatía*
– in the balcony _____	Θέλουμε...θέσεις στον εξώστη *théloome...thésis ston exósti*
– box seats _____	Θέλουμε...θέσεις στο θεωρείο *théloome...thésis sto theorío*
– a table at the front _____	Θέλουμε...θέσεις/ένα τραπέζι μπροστά *théloome...thésis/éna trapézi brostá*
– in the middle _____	Θέλουμε...θέσεις/ένα τραπέζι στη μέση *théloome...thésis/éna trapézi sti mési*
– at the back _____	Θέλουμε...θέσεις/ένα τραπέζι πίσω *théloome...thésis/éna trapézi píso*
Could I reserve...seats for __ the...o'clock performance?	Μπορώ να κλείσω...θέσεις για την παράσταση στις...; *boró na klíso...thésis ya timbarástasi stis...?*
Are there any seats left ____ for tonight?	Υπάρχουν ακόμα εισιτήρια για απόψε; *ipárchoon akóma isitírya ya apópse?*
How much is a ticket? _____	Πόσο κοστίζει το εισιτήριο; *póso kostízi to isitíryo?*
When can I pick the _____ tickets up?	Πότε μπορώ να πάρω τα εισιτήρια; *póte boró na páro ta isitírya?*
I've got a reservation _____	Έχω κλείσει θέσεις *écho klísi thésis*
My name's... _____	Το όνομά μου είναι... *to ónomámoo íne...*

Για ποιά παράσταση θέλετε να_____ κλείσετε εισιτήρια;	Which performance do you want to reserve for?
Πού θέλετε να καθίσετε;_____	Where would you like to sit?
Όλα πουλήθηκαν_____	Everything's sold out
Υπάρχουν μόνο θέσεις για όρθιους _____	It's standing room only
Υπάρχουν μόνο θέσεις στον εξώστη _____	We've only got balcony seats left
Υπάρχουν μόνο θέσεις στη γαλαρία _____	We've only got seats left in the top balcony
Υπάρχουν μόνο θέσεις στην πλατεία_____	We've only got orchestra seats left
Υπάρχουν μόνο θέσεις μπροστά _____	We've only got seats left at the front
Υπάρχουν μόνο θέσεις πίσω_____	We've only got seats left at the back
Πόσες θέσεις θέλετε; _____	How many seats would you like?
Πρέπει να πάρετε τα εισιτήρια πριν _____ από τις...	You'll have to pick up the tickets before...o'clock
Τα εισιτήριά σας, παρακαλώ_____	Tickets, please
Ορίστε, η θέση σας _____	This is your seat

At the Tourist Information Center

11

Sports

12 **S**ports

12 .1 **S**porting questions

Where can we... around here?	Πού μπορούμε να...εδώ; *poo boróome na...edhó?*
Is there a... around here?	Υπάρχει ένα...εδώ κοντά; *ipárchi éna...edhó kondá?*
Can I hire a...here?	Μπορώ να νοικιάσω ένα...; *boró na nikyáso éna...?*
Can I take...lessons?	Γίνονται μαθήματα...; *yínonde mathímata...?*
How much is that per hour/per day/a turn?	Πόσο κοστίζει την ώρα/τη μέρα/τη φορά; *póso kostízi tin óra/ti méra/ti forá?*
Do I need a permit for that?	Χρειάζομαι μια άδεια για αυτό; *chriázome mya ádhya yavtó?*
Where can I get the permit?	Πού μπορώ να βγάλω μια τέτοια άδεια; *poo boró na vghálo mya tétya ádhya?*

12 .2 **B**y the waterfront

Is it a long way to the sea still?	Η θάλασσα είναι ακόμα μακριά; *i thálasa íne akóma makriá?*
Is there a...around here?	Υπάρχει κι ένα...εδώ κοντά; *ipárchi kyéna ... edhó kondá?*
– an outdoor/indoor/ public swimming pool	Υπάρχει και μια πισίνα εδώ κοντά; *ipárchi ke mya pisína edhó kondá?*
– a sandy beach	Υπάρχει και μια παραλια εδώ κοντά; *ipárchi ke mya paralía edhó kondá?*
– a nudist beach	Υπάρχει και μια πλαζ για γυμνιστές εδώ κοντά; *ipárchi ke mya plaz ya yimnastés edhó kondá?*
– dock	Υπάρχει και μια μαρίνα εδώ κοντά; *ipárchi ke mya marína edhó kondá?*
Are there any rocks here?	Εχει και βράχους εδώ; *éhi ke vráchoos edhó?*
When's high/low tide?	Τι ώρα έχει παλίρροια/άμπωτη; *ti óra éhi palíria/ámboti?*
What's the water temperature?	Τι θερμοκρασία έχει το νερό; *ti thermokrasía éhi to neró?*
Is it (very) deep here?	Είναι (πολύ) βαθιά εδώ; *íne (poli) vathyá edhó?*
Can you stand here?	Πατώνεις εδώ; *patónis edhó?*
Is it safe (for children) to swim here?	Είναι ασφαλές το κολύμπι εδώ (για παιδιά); *íne asfalés to kolímbi edhó (ya pedhyá)?*
Are there any currents?	Εχει ρεύματα εδώ; *éhi révmata edhó?*
Are there any rapids/ waterfalls in this river?	Αυτό το ποτάμι έχει καταρράχτες; *aftó to potámi éhi katarráchtes?*
What does that flag/ buoy mean?	Τι σημαίνει εκείνη η σημαία/σημαδούρα εκεί; *ti siméni ekíni i siméa/simadhóora ekí?*

Is there a lifeguard on duty here?	Έχει εδώ κανένα ακτοφύλακα που να προσέχει;
	éhi edhó kanéna aktofílaka poo na proséhi?
Are dogs allowed here?___	Επιτρέπονται εδώ τα σκυλιά;
	epitréponde edhó ta skilyá?
Is camping on the beach allowed?	Επιτρέπεται η κατασκήνωση εδώ στην παραλία;
	epitrépete i kataskínosi edhó stimbaralía?
Are we allowed to build a fire here?	Επιτρέπεται να ανάβει κανείς εδώ φωτιά;
	epitrépete nanávi kanís edhó fotyá?

ΑΠΑΓΟΡΕΥΕΤΑΙ ΤΟ ΚΟΛΥΜΠΙ	ΑΠΑΓΟΡΕΥΕΤΑΙ ΤΟ ΨΑΡΕΜΑ	ΚΙΝΔΥΝΟΣ
no swimming	no fishing	danger
ΑΠΑΓΟΡΕΥΕΤΑΙ ΤΟ ΣΕΡΦΙΝΓΚ	ΕΠΙΤΡΕΠΕΤΑΙ ΤΟ ΨΑΡΕΜΑ	ΜΟΝΟ ΜΕ ΑΔΕΙΑ
no surfing	fishing permitted	permits only

12.3 Water sports

Can I take water ski lessons here?	Μπορώ να κάνω εδώ θαλάσσιο σκι;
	boró na káno edhó thalásyo ski?
Can I get diving instruction here?	Μπορώ να κάνω μαθήματα κατάδυσης;
	boró na káno mathímata katadhísis?
How large are the groups?	Πόσο μεγάλα είναι τα γκρουπ;
	póso meghála íne ta groop?
What language are the classes in?	Σε ποια γλώσσα παραδίνονται τα μαθήματα;
	se pya ghlósa paradhínonde ta mathímata?
Can I rent diving equipment here?	Μπορώ να νοικιάσω εδώ εξαρτήματα κατάδυσης;
	boró na nikyáso edhó exartímata katádhisis?
Can I dive here?	Μπορώ να κάνω εδώ κατάδυση;
	boró na káno edhó katádhisi?

Sports

Sickness

Sickness

.1 Call (get) the doctor

Could you call/get a _____ doctor quickly, please?	Παρακαλώ, καλέστε/ειδοποιήστε γρήγορα ένα γιατρό
	parakaló, kaléste/idhopiíste ghríghora éna yatró
When does the doctor _____ have office hours?	Πότε δέχεται ο γιατρός;
	póte dhéchete o yatrós?
When can the doctor _____ come?	Πότε μπορεί να έρθει ο γιατρός;
	póte borí na érthi o yatrós?
I'd like to make an _____ appointment to see the doctor	Μπορείτε να μου κλείσετε ένα ραντεβού με το γιατρό;
	boríte na moo klísete éna randevóo me to yatró?
I've got an appointment ___ to see the doctor at...	Έχω ένα ραντεβού με το γιατρό στις...
	écho éna randevóo me to yatró stis ...
Which doctor/pharmacy ___ has night/weekend duty?	Ποιος γιατρός/ποιό φαρμακείο διανυκτερεύει/διανυκτερεύει το Σαββατοκύριακο;
	pyos yatrós/pyo farmakío dhianikterévi/dhianikterévi to savatokíryako?

.2 Patient's ailments

I don't feel well _____	Δεν αισθάνομαι καλά
	dhen esthánome kalá
I'm dizzy_____	Ζαλίζομαι
	zalízome
– ill_____	Είμαι άρρωστος/άρρωστη
	íme árostos/árosti
– sick _____	Ανακατεύεται το στομάχι μου
	anakatévete to stomáchimoo
I've got a cold_____	Είμαι κρυωμένος/κρυωμένη
	íme krioménos/krioméni
It hurts here _____	Πονάω εδώ
	ponáo edhó
I've been throwing up ____	Έκανα εμετό
	ékana emetó
I've got... _____	Μ' ενοχλεί...
	menochlí...
I'm running a _____ temperature of...degrees	Έχω...βαθμούς πυρετό
	écho...vathmóos piretó
I've been stung by_____ a wasp	Με τσίμπησε μια σφήκα
	me tsíbise mya sfíka
I've been stung by an_____ insect	Με τσίμπησε ένα έντομο
	me tsíbise éna éndomo
I've been bitten by _____ a dog	Με δάγκωσε ένας σκύλος
	me dhángose énas skílos
I've been stung by_____ a jellyfish	Με τσίμπησε μια μέδουσα;
	me tsímbise mya medhóosa
I've been bitten by _____ a snake	Με δάγκωσε ένα φίδι
	me dhángose éna fídhi

Sickness

13

I've been bitten by an animal	Με δάγκωσε ένα ζώο
	me dhángose éna zó-o
I've cut myself	Κόπηκα
	kópika
I've burned myself	Κάηκα
	káika
I've grazed myself	Γρατσουνίστηκα
	ghratsoonístika
I've had a fall	Έπεσα
	épesa
I've sprained my ankle	Στραμπούληξα τον αστράγαλό μου
	strambóolixa ton astrághalómoo
I've come for the morning-after pill	Έρχομαι για το μόρνιγκ-άφτερ-χάπι
	érchome ya to morning-áfter-chápi

.3 The consultation

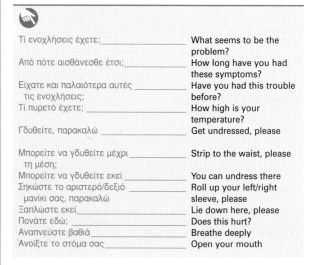

Τί ενοχλήσεις έχετε;	What seems to be the problem?
Από πότε αισθάνεσθε έτσι;	How long have you had these symptoms?
Είχατε και παλαιότερα αυτές τις ενοχλήσεις;	Have you had this trouble before?
Τί πυρετό έχετε;	How high is your temperature?
Γδυθείτε, παρακαλώ	Get undressed, please
Μπορείτε να γδυθείτε μέχρι τη μέση;	Strip to the waist, please
Μπορείτε να γδυθείτε εκεί	You can undress there
Σηκώστε το αριστερό/δεξιό μανίκι σας, παρακαλώ	Roll up your left/right sleeve, please
Ξαπλώστε εκεί	Lie down here, please
Πονάτε εδώ;	Does this hurt?
Αναπνεύστε βαθιά	Breathe deeply
Ανοίξτε το στόμα σας	Open your mouth

Patient's medical history

I'm a diabetic	Είμαι διαβητικός
	íme dhiavitikós
I have a heart condition	Είμαι καρδιακός
	íme kardhiakós
I have asthma	Έχω άσθμα
	écho ásthma
I'm allergic to...	Είμαι αλλεργικός σε...
	íme aleryikós se...
I'm...months pregnant	Είμαι...μηνών έγκυος
	íme...minón éngios
I'm on a diet	Κάνω δίαιτα
	káno dhíeta

I'm on medication/the pill __	Παίρνω φάρμακα/το χάπι	
	pérno fármaka/to chápi	
I've had a heart attack _____	Εχω ξαναπάθει καρδιακή προσβολή	
once before	*écho xanapáthi kardhiakí prosvolí*	
I've had a(n)...operation ___	Εκανα εγχείρηση στο...	
	ékana enchírisi sto...	
I've been ill recently _____	Πρόσφατα ήμουν άρρωστος/άρρωστη	
	prósfata ímoon árostos/árosti	
I've got an ulcer_____	Εχω στομαχικό έλκος	
	écho stomachikó élkos	
I've got my period_____	Εχω περίοδο	
	écho períodho	

Είστε αλλεργικός σε κάτι;	_____	Do you have any allergies?
Παίρνετε φάρμακα	_____	Are you on any medication?
Κάνετε δίαιτα;	_____	Are you on a diet?
Είστε έγκυος;	_____	Are you pregnant?
Είστε εμβολιασμένος κατά του τέτανου...;	_____	Have you had a tetanus injection?

The diagnosis

Δεν είναι τίποτα σοβαρό	_____	It's nothing serious
Εχετε σπάσει...το/τη...σας	_____	Your...is broken
Εχετε στραμπουλήξει...το/τη...σας	_____	You've got a strained/sprained...
Εχετε σκίσει...το/τη...σας	_____	You've got (a) torn...
Εχετε μια φλεγμονή	_____	You've got an infection
Εχετε σκωληκοειδίτιδα	_____	You've got appendicitis
Εχετε βρογχίτιδα	_____	You've got bronchitis
Εχετε ένα αφροδίσιο νόσημα	_____	You've got a venereal disease
Εχετε γρίππη	_____	You've got the flu
Πάθατε καρδιακή προσβολή	_____	You've had a heart attack
Εχετε ίωση/βακτηριακή μόλυνση	_____	You've got an infection (viral..., bacterial...)
Εχετε πνευμονία	_____	You've got pneumonia
Εχετε έλκος	_____	You've got an ulcer
Εχετε πάθει νευροκαβαλίκεμα	_____	You've pulled a muscle
Εχετε κολπική μόλυνση	_____	You've got a vaginal infection
Πάθατε τροφική δηλητηρίαση	_____	You've got food poisoning
Εχετε πάθει ηλίαση	_____	You've got sunstroke
Είστε αλλεργικός στο/στη...	_____	You're allergic to...
Είστε έγκυος	_____	You're pregnant
Θέλω να κάνω εξέταση του αίματός σας/των ούρων σας/των κοπράνων σας	_____	I'd like to have your blood/urine/stools tested

Sickness

13

99

Πρέπει να ραφτεί _____	It needs stitching
Σας στέλνω σ' ένα ειδικό/σ' ένα _____ νοσοκομείο	I'm referring you to a specialist/sending you to the hospital
Πρέπει να κάνουμε ακτινογραφίες_____	You'll need to have some x-rays taken
Πρέπει να περιμένετε δύο _____ λεπτά στην αίθουσα αναμονής	Could you wait in the waiting room, please?
Πρέπει να εγχειρισθείτε _____	You'll need an operation

Is it contagious?_____	Είναι κολλητικό; íne kolitikó?
How long do I have to _____ stay...?	Πόσο καιρό πρέπει να μείνω σε...; póso kyeró prépi na míno se...?
– in bed _____	Πόσο καιρό πρέπει να μείνω στο κρεβάτι; póso kyeró prépi na míno sto kreváti?
– in the hospital_____	Πόσο καιρό πρέπει να μείνω στο νοσοκομείο; póso kyeró prépi na míno sto nosokomío?
Do I have to go on _____ a special diet?	Πρέπει να κάνω καμιά δίαιτα; prépi na káno kamyá dhíeta?
Am I allowed to travel? ____	Μπορώ να ταξιδέψω; boró na taxidhépso?
Can I make a new _____ appointment?	Μπορώ να κλείσω ένα άλλο ραντεβού; boró na klíso éna álo randevóo?
When do I have to_____ come back?	Πότε πρέπει να ξανάρθω; póte prépi na xanártho?
I'll come back _____ tomorrow	Θα ξανάρθω αύριο tha xanártho ávrio

| Πρέπει να ξαναρθείτε αύριο/σε...μέρες _____ | Come back tomorrow/in...days' time |

🔟 .4 Medication and prescriptions

How do I take this _____ medicine?	Πώς πρέπει να το παίρνω αυτό το φάρμακο; pos prépi na to pérno aftó to fármako?
How many pills/drops/_____ injections/spoonfuls/ tablets each time?	Πόσες κάψουλες/σταγόνες/ενέσεις/πόσα κουταλάκια/χάπια τη φορά; póses kapsóoles/staghónes/enésis/pósa kootalákya/chápya ti forá?
How many times a day? ___	Πόσες φορές την ημέρα; póses forés tin iméra?
I've forgotten my_____ medication. At home I take...	Ξέχασα τα φάρμακά μου. Σπίτι χρησιμοποιώ... xéchasa ta fármakámoo. spíti chrisimopió ...
Could you write a _____ prescription for me?	Μπορείτε να μου δώσετε μια συνταγή; boríte na moo dhósete mya sintayí?

Θα σας δώσω αντιβιοτικά/ένα σιρόπι/ _____ έναηρεμιστικό/ένα παυσίπονο	I'm prescribing antibiotics/a mixture/a tranquilizer/painkillers
Πρέπει να ξεκουραστείτε _____	Have lots of rest
Καλύτερα να μην βγείτε έξω _____	Stay indoors
Πρέπει να μείνετε στο κρεβάτι _____	Stay in bed

αλείφω	κατά τη διάρκεια...	παίρνω
rub on	ημερών	take
αλοιφή	for...days	πριν από κάθε
ointment	καταπίνω ολόκληρο	γεύμα
αυτά τα φάρμακα	swallow whole	before every meal
επηρεάζουν την	κάψουλες	σταγόνες
ικανότητα οδήγησης	pills	drops
this medication	κουτάλια/κουταλάκια	τελειώνω τη θεραπεία
impairs your	spoonfuls	finish the course
driving	(tablespoons/	of treatment
διαλύω σε νερό	teaspoons)	...φορές το
dissolve in water	μόνο για εξωτερική	μερόνυχτο
ενέσεις	χρήση	...times a day
injections	not for internal	χάπια
κάθε...ώρες	use	tablets
every...hours		

.5 At the dentist's

Do you know a good _____ dentist?	Ξέρετε ένα καλό οδοντογιατρό; *xérete éna kaló odhondoyatró?*
Could you make a _____ dentist's appointment for me? It's urgent	Μπορείτε να μου κλείσετε ραντεβού με τον οδοντογιατρό; Είναι επείγον *boríte na moo klísete randevóo me ton odhondoyatró? íne epíghon*
Can I come in today, _____ please?	Μπορώ να έρθω σήμερα, παρακαλώ; *boró na értho símera, parakaló?*
I have (terrible) _____ toothache	Εχω (φοβερό) πονόδοντο *écho (foveró) ponódhondo*
Could you prescribe/ _____ give me a painkiller?	Μπορείτε να μου γράψετε/δώσετε ένα παυσίπονο; *boríte na moo ghrápsete/dhósete éna pafsípono?*
A piece of my tooth _____ has broken off	Εσπασε ένα κομματάκι του δοντιού μου/του τραπεζίτη μου *éspase éna komatáki too dondyóomoo/too trapezítimoo*
My filling's come out _____	Βγήκε ένα σφράγισμα *vyíke éna sfráyizma*
I've got a broken crown _____	Εσπασε η κορόνα μου *éspase i koróna moo*
I'd like/I don't want a _____ local anaesthetic	Θέλω/δε θέλω τοπική αναισθησία *thélo/dhe thélo topikí anesthisía*

Sickness

13

Can you do a temporary ___
repair job?
I don't want this tooth ___
pulled

My dentures are broken. ___
Can you fix them?

Μπορείτε να με βοηθήσετε προσωρινά;
boríte na me voithísete prosoriná?
Δε θέλω να το βγάλετε αυτόν τον
τραπεζίτη
dhe thélo na to vghálete aftón ton trapezíti

Η μασέλα μου έσπασε. Μπορείτε να τη
φτιάξετε;
i masélamoo éspase. boríte na ti ftyáxete?

Ποιό δόντι/ποιός τραπεζίτης σας ___ πονάει;	Which tooth/molar hurts?
Έχετε ένα απόστημα ___	You've got an abscess
Πρέπει να κάνω απονεύρωση ___	I'll have to do a root canal
Θα σας κάνω τοπική αναισθησία ___	I'm giving you a local anaesthetic
Πρέπει να βουλώσω/βγάλω/λιμάρω ___ αυτό το...	I'll have to fill/pull/file this tooth down
Πρέπει να τρυπήσω το δόντι ___	I'll have to drill
Ανοίξτε το στόμα ___	Open wide, please
Κλείστε το στόμα ___	Close your mouth, please
Ξεπλύντε το ___	Rinse, please
Πονάει ακόμα; ___	Does it hurt still?

In trouble

14 .1 Asking for help

Help!	Βοήθεια!	voíthya!
Fire!	Φωτιά!	fotyá!
Police!	Αστυνομία!	astinomía!
Quick!	Γρήγορα!	ghríghora!
Danger!	Κίνδυνος!	kíndhinos!
Watch out!	Προσοχή!	prosohí!
Stop!	Σταματήστε!	stamatíste!
Be careful!	Προσοχή!	prosohí!
Don't!	Μη!	mi!
Let go!	Αφήστε το!	afiséto
Stop that thief!	Πιάστε τον κλέφτη!	pyáste tongléfti!
Could you help me, please?	Μπορείτε να με βοηθήσετε;	boríte na me voithísete?
Where's the police station/emergency exit/fire escape?	Πού είναι το αστυνομικό τμήμα/η έξοδος κινδύνου;	poo íne to astinomikó tmíma/i éxodhos kindhínoo?
Where's the nearest fire extinguisher?	Πού βρίσκεται ένας πυροσβεστήρας;	poo vrískete énas pirosvestíras?
Call the fire department!	Ειδοποιείστε την πυροσβεστική υπηρεσία!	idhopiíste timbirosvestikí ipiresía!
Call the police!	Τηλεφωνήστε στην αστυνομία!	tilefoníste stin astinomía!
Call an ambulance!	Ειδοποιήστε ένα ασθενοφόρο!	idhopiíste éna asthenofóro!
Where's the nearest phone?	Πού υπάρχει ένα τηλέφωνο;	poo ipárchi éna tiléfono?
Could I use your phone?	Μπορώ να χρησιμοποιήσω το τηλέφωνό σας;	boró na chrisimopiíso to tiléfonósas?
What's the emergency number?	Ποιός είναι ο αριθμός του συναγερμού;	pyos íne o arithmós too sinayermóo?
What's the number for the police?	Ποιός είναι ο αριθμός της αστυνομίας;	pyos íne o arithmós tis astinomías?

I've lost my purse/_____ wallet	Εχασα το πορτοφόλι μου *échasa to portofólimoo*
I lost my...yesterday _____	Ξέχασα χτες το...μου *xéchasa chtes to...moo*
I left my...here _____	Άφησα εδώ το...μου *áfisa edhó to...moo*
Did you find my...? _____	Μήπως βρήκατε το...μου; *mípos vríkate to...moo?*
It was right here_____	Ήταν εδώ *tan edhó*
It's quite valuable _____	Είναι πολύτιμο *íne polítimo*
Where's the Lost _____ and Found office?	Πού βρίσκεται το γραφείο ευρεθέντων αντικειμένων; *poo vrískete to ghrafío evrethéndon andikiménon?*

There's been an accident __	Εγινε ένα ατύχημα *éyine éna atíhima*
Someone's fallen into _____ the water	Κάποιος έπεσε στο νερό *kápyos épese sto neró*
There's a fire_____	Ξέσπασε πυρκαγιά *xéspase pirkayá*
Is anyone hurt? _____	Υπάρχουν τραυματίες; *ipárchoon travmatíes?*
Some people have _____ been/no one's been injured	(Δεν) υπάρχουν τραυματίες *(dhen) ipárchoon travmatíes*
There's someone in _____ the car/train still	Εχει και άλλον έναν στο αυτοκίνητο/στο τρένο *éhi ke álo énan sto aftokínito/sto tréno*
It's not too bad. Don't_____ worry	Δεν είναι και τόσο άσχημα. Μην ανησυχείτε *dhen íne ke tóso áschima. min anisihíte*
Leave everything the _____ way it is, please	Μην κουνήσετε τίποτα *min koonísete típota*
I want to talk to the_____ police first	Θέλω πρώτα να μιλήσω με την αστυνομία *thélo próta na milíso me tin astinomía*
I want to take a _____ photo first	Θέλω πρώτα να βγάλω μία φωτογραφία *thélo próta na vghálo mya fotoghrafía*
Here's my name_____ and address	Να το όνομά μου και η διεύθυνσή μου *na to ónomámoo ke i dhiéfthinsímoo*
Could I have your _____ name and address?	Μου δίνετε το όνομά σας και τη διεύθυνσή σας; *moo dhínete to ónomásas ke ti dhiéfthinsísas?*
Could I see some_____ identification/your insurance papers?	Μπορώ να δω την ταυτότητά σας/τα χαρτιά της ασφάλειάς σας; *boró na dho tin taftótitásas/ta chartyá tis asfalyás sas?*
Will you act as a _____ witness?	Θέλετε να εμφανιστείτε ως μάρτυρας; *thélete na emfanistíte os mártiras?*
I need the details for _____ the insurance	Χρειάζομαι τα στοιχεία για την ασφάλεια *chriázome ta stihía ya tin asfálya*

In trouble

Are you insured? _____ Είστε ασφαλισμένος/ασφαλισμένη;
íste asfalizménos/asfalizméni?

Third party or _____ Απλή ή μικτή ασφάλεια;
all inclusive? *aplí i miktí asfálya?*

Could you sign here, _____ Παρακαλώ, να υπογράψετε εδώ
please? *parakaló, na ipoghrápsete edhó*

I've been robbed _____ Μ' έκλεψαν
méklepsan

My...has been stolen _____ Έκλεψαν το...μου
éklepsan to...moo

My car's been _____ Παραβίασαν το αυτοκίνητό μου
broken into *paravíasan to aftokínitómoo*

I've lost my child/ _____ Έχασα το παιδί μου/τη γιαγιά μου
grandmother *échasa to pedhímoo/ti yayámoo*

Could you help me _____ Μπορείτε να με βοηθήσετε να το/τη βρω;
find him/her? *boríte na me voithísete na to/ti vro?*

Have you seen a _____ Μήπως είδατε ένα μικρό παιδί;
small child? *mípos ídhate éna mikró pedhí?*

He's/she's...years old _____ Είναι...χρονών
íne...chronó

He's/she's got _____ Έχει...κοντά/μακριά/ξανθά/κόκκινα/
short/long/blond/red/ καστανά/μαύρα/γκρίζα/σγουρά/ίσια/
brown/black/gray/curly/ κατσαρά μαλλιά
straight/frizzy hair *éhi kondá/makryá/xanthá/kókina/kastaná/
mávra/gríza/zghoorá/ ísya/ katsará malyá*

with a ponytail _____ με αλογοουρά
me aloghó-oorá

with braids _____ με κοτσίδες
me kotsídhes

in a bun _____ με κότσο
me kótso

He's/she's got _____ Τα μάτια του/της είναι
blue/brown/green eyes μπλε/καστανά/πράσινα
ta mátya too/tis íne ble/kastaná/prásina

He's wearing swimming ___ Φοράει μαγιό/παπούτσια ορειβασίας
trunks/hiking boots *forái mayó/papóotsya orivalsaís*

with/without glasses/ _____ με/χωρίς γυαλιά/τσάντα
a bag *me/chorís yalyá/tsánda*

tall/short_____ ψηλός/κοντός
psilós/kondós

This is a photo of _____ Να μια φωτογραφία του/της
him/her *na mya fotohrafía too/tis*

He/she must be lost _____ Μάλλον έχασε το δρόμο
málon échase to dhrómo

An arrest

Τα χαρτιά του αυτοκινήτου σας, _____ παρακαλώ	Your registration papers, please
Τρέχατε πολύ _____	You were speeding
Παρκάρατε παράνομα _____	You're not allowed to park here
Δε βάλατε λεφτά στο παρκόμετρο _____	You haven't put money in the meter
Τα φώτα σας δε λειτουργούν _____	Your lights aren't working
Θα πληρώσετε πρόστιμο ... δραχμών _____	That's a...drachma fine
Θέλετε να πληρώσετε αμέσως; _____	Do you want to pay now?
Πρέπει να πληρώσετε αμέσως _____	You'll have to pay now

I don't speak Greek _____	Δε μιλάω ελληνικά *dhe miláo eliniká*
I didn't see the sign _____	Δεν είδα εκείνη την πινακίδα *dhen ídha ekíni timbinakídha*
I don't understand _____ what it says	Δεν καταλαβαίνω τι λέει εδώ *dhengkatalavéno ti léi edhó*
I was only doing... _____ kilometers an hour	Οδηγούσα μόνο ... χιλιόμετρα την ώρα *odhighóosa móno ... hilyómetra tin óra*
I'll have my car checked ___	Θα πάω το αυτοκίνητό μου στο συνεργείο *tha páo to aftokínitómoo sto sineryío*
I was blinded by _____ oncoming lights	Τυφλώθηκα από ένα αυτοκίνητο που ερχόταν από την αντίθετη κατεύθυνση *tiflóthika apó éna aftokínito poo erchótan apó tin andítheti katéfthinsi*

At the police station

I want to report a _____ collision/missing person/rape	Ήρθα για να αναφέρω μια σύγκρουση/μια απώλεια/ένα βιασμό *írtha ya na anféro mya síngroosi/mya apólya/éna viazmó*
Could you make out _____ a report, please?	Μπορείτε να κάνετε αναφορά για το αυτόφωρο; *boríte na kánete anaforá ya to aftóforo?*
Could I have a copy _____ for the insurance?	Μπορείτε να μου δώσετε ένα αντίγραφο για την ασφάλεια; *boríte na moo dhósete éna andígrafo ya tin asfálya?*
I've lost everything _____	Έχασα τα πάντα *échasa ta pánda*
I've no money; I don't _____ know what to do	Τα λεφτά μου τελείωσαν, δεν ξέρω τι να κάνω *ta leftámoo telíosan, dhengxéro ti na káno*
Could you lend me a _____ little cash?	Μπορείτε να μου δανείσετε λίγα λεφτά; *boríte na moo dhanísete lígha leftá?*

In trouble

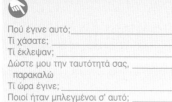

Πού έγινε αυτό; _____	Where did it happen?
Τί χάσατε; _____	What's missing?
Τί έκλεψαν; _____	What's been taken?
Δώστε μου την ταυτότητά σας, _____ παρακαλώ	Could I see some identification?
Τί ώρα έγινε; _____	What time did it happen?
Ποιοί ήταν μπλεγμένοι σ' αυτό; _____	Who was involved?
Υπάρχουν μάρτυρες; _____	Are there any witnesses?
Να συμπληρώσετε αυτό, παρακαλώ _____	Fill this out, please
Υπογράψτε εδώ, παρακαλώ _____	Sign here, please
Θέλετε ένα διερμηνέα; _____	Do you want an interpreter?

I'd like an interpreter _____ Θα ήθελα ένα διερμηνέα
tha íthela éna dhierminéa

I'm innocent _____ Είμαι αθώος
íme athó-os

I don't know anything about it _____ Δεν ξέρω τίποτα για αυτό
dhengxéro típota yaftó

I want to speak to someone _____ Θέλω να μιλήσω με κάποιον από ...
thélo na milíso me kápyon apó ...

I want to speak to someone from the American consulate _____ Θέλω να μιλήσω με κάποιον από το αμερικανικο προξενείο
thélo na milíso me kápyon apó to amerikániko proxenío

I need to see someone from the American embassy _____ Θέλω να μιλήσω με κάποιον από τη αμερικανικη πρεσβεία
thélo na milíso me kápyon apó ti amerikánikí prezvía

I want a lawyer who speaks English _____ Θέλω ένα δικηγόρο που να μιλάει ...
thélo éna dhikighóro poo na milái ...

In trouble

14

15

Word list

Word list English - Greek

● **This word list** is intended to supplement the previous chapters. Nouns are usually accompanied by the Greek definite article in order to indicate whether the word is masculine (o), feminine (η), or neuter (το). In the case of a plural noun the form of the definite article will be οι for masculine and feminine nouns and τα for neuter nouns.

In a number of cases, words not contained in this list can be found elsewhere in this book, namely alongside the diagrams of the car, the bicycle and the tent. Many food terms can be found in the Greek-English list in 4.7.

A

a little	λίγο	lígho
about	περίπου	perípoo
above	πάνω	páno
abroad	το εξωτερικό	to exoterikó
accident	το ατύχημα	to atíhima
according	κατά	katá
adder	η οχιά	i ochyá
addition	η πρόσθεση	i prósthesi
address	η διεύθυνση	i dhiéfthinsi
admission	η είσοδος	i ísodhos
admission price	η είσοδος	i ísodhos
adult	μεγάλος	meghálos
advice	η συμβουλή	i simvoolí
afraid (I am)	φοβάμαι	fováme
after, afterwards	μετά	metá
aftershave	το αφτερ-σέιβ	to áfter-séiv
afternoon	το απόγευμα	to apóyevma
again	ξανά	xaná
against	ενάντια σε	enándya se
age	η ηλικία	i ilikía
AIDS	ΕΙΤΖ	éitz
air mattress	το αερόστρωμα	to aeróstroma
air conditioning	ο κλιματισμός	o klimatizmós
airplane	το αεροπλάνο	to aeropláno
airport	το αεροδρόμιο	to aerodhrómio
airsickness bag	η σακούλα για εμετό	i sakóola ya emetó
alarm	ο συναγερμός	o sinayermós
alarm clock	το ξυπνητήρι	to xipnitíri
alcohol	το αλκοόλ	to alkoól
allergic	αλλεργικός	aleryikós
alone/only	μόνος	mónos
alter	αλλάζω	alázo
always	πάντα	pánda
ambulance	το ασθενοφόρο	to asthenofóro
America	Αμερική	amérikí
American	αμερικανικος	amerikánikos
amount	το ποσό	to posó
amusement park	το λούνα παρκ	to lóonapark
anaesthetize	ναρκώνω	narkóno
anchovy	η αντσούγια	i antsóoya
ancient/very old	αρχαίος	archéos
angry	θυμωμένος	thimoménos
animal	το ζώο	to zóo
ankle	ο αστράγαλος	o astrághalos

answer	η απάντηση	*i apándisi*
ant	το μυρμήγκι	*to mirmíngi*
antibiotics	τα αντιβιοτικά	*ta andiviotiká*
antifreeze	το αντιψυκτικό	*to andipsiktikó*
antique (an)	η αντίκα	*i antíka*
anus	ο πρωκτός	*o proktós*
apartment	το διαμέρισμα	*to dhiamérizma*
apartment building	η πολυκατοικία	*i polikatikía*
apologies	συγγνώμη	*sighnómi*
appetizer	το ορεκτικό	*to orektikó*
apple juice	ο χυμός μήλων	*o himós mílon*
apple	το μήλο	*to mílo*
apple sauce	ο πολτός μήλων	*o poltós mílon*
apple pie	η μηλόπιτα	*i milópita*
appointment/date	το ραντεβού	*to randevóo*
apricot	το βερίκοκο	*to veríkoko*
April	ο Απρίλιος	*o aprílios*
archbishop	ο αρχιεπίσκοπος	*o archiepískopos*
architecture	η αρχιτεκτονική	*i architektonikí*
area code	το κωδικό	*to gódhiko*
arm	το χέρι	*to héri*
arrive	φτάνω	*ftáno*
arrow	το βέλος	*to vélos*
art	η τέχνη	*i téchni*
artery	η αρτηρία	*i artiría*
artichokes	οι αγγινάρες	*i angináres*
artificial	η τεχνητή αναπνοή	*i technití anapnoí*
ashtray	το τασάκι	*to tasáki*
ask (for)	ζητώ	*zitó*
ask (question)	ρωτάω	*rotáo*
asparagus	τα σπαράγγια	*ta sparángya*
aspirin	η ασπιρίνη	*i aspiríni*
at home	σπίτι	*spíti*
August	ο Αύγουστος	*o ávghoostos*
automatic (adj.)	αυτόματος	*aftómatos*
automatic (noun)	το αυτόματο	*to aftómato*
autumn	το φθινόπωρο	*to fthinóporo*
awake	ξύπνιος	*xípnios*
awning	το αλεξήλιο	*to alexílyo*

B

baby	το μωρό	*to moró*
baby food	το φαγητό για μωρά	*to fayitó ya morá*
baby's bottle	το μπιμπερό	*to biberó*
babysitter	η μπέιμπυ σίτερ	*i béibi-síter*
bachelor	ο εργένης	*o eryénis*
back	η πλάτη	*i pláti*
back, at the	πίσω	*píso*
backpack	ο σάκος	*o sákos*
bacterial infection	η βακτηριακή μόλυνση	*i vaktiriakí mólinsi*
bad (serious)	σοβαρός	*sovarós*
bad	κακός	*kakós*
bakery	το αρτοπωλείο/ο φούρνος	*to artopolío/o fóornos*
balcony (in theater)	ο εξώστης	*o exóstis*
balcony	το μπαλκόνι	*to balkóni*
ball	η μπάλα	*i bála*

ballet	το μπαλέτο	to baléto
banana	η μπανάνα	i banána
bandage	ο επίδεσμος	o epídhezmos
Bandaids	ο λευκοπλάστης	o lefkoplástis
bangs (hair)	η φράντζα	i frándza
bank	η τράπεζα	i trápeza
bank card	η τραπεζική κάρτα	i trapezikí kárta
bank (river)	η όχθη	i óchthi
bar (café)	το μπαρ	to bar
bar (in one's room)	το μπαρ	to bar
barbecue	το μπαρμπεκιού	to barbekyóo
barber	ο κουρέας	o kooréas
basketball	το μπάσκετ	to básket
bath/swim	το μπάνιο	to bányo
bath	το μπάνιο	to bányo
bath foam	το αφρόλουτρο μπάνιου	to afrólootro bányoo
bath towel	η πετσέτα	i petséta
bathing cap	η σκούφια του μπάνιου	i skóofya too bányoo
battery	η μπαταρία	i bataría
beach	η πλαζ	i plaz
beans	τα φασόλια	ta fasólya
beautiful	όμορφος	ómorfos
beauty parlor	το ινστιτούτο καλλονής	to institóoto kalonís
bed	το κρεβάτι	to kreváti
bee	η μέλισσα	i mélissa
beef	το βοδινό κρέας	to vodhinó kréas
beer	η μπύρα	i bíra
beet	το παντζάρι	to padzári
begin	αρχίζω	archízo
beginner	ο αρχάριος	o archáryos
behind	πίσω από	píso apó
belly	η κοιλιά	i kilyá
belly ache	ο κοιλόπονος	o kilóponos
beloved	αγαπημένος	aghapiménos
belt	η ζώνη	i zóni
bicarbonate of soda	η σόδα	i sódha
bicycle	το ποδήλατο	to podhílato
bicycle pump	η τρόμπα	i trómba
big	μεγάλος	meghálos
bikini	το μπικίνι	to bikíni
bill	ο λογαριασμός	o loghariazmós
billiards	το μπιλιάρδο	to bilyárdho
biro	το στυλό	to stiló
birthday	τα γενέθλια	ta yenéthlia
birthday (it's my)	έχω γενέθλια	écho yenéthlia
bite (verb)	δαγκώνω	dhangóno
bitter (adj.)	πικρός	pikrós
black	μαύρος	mávros
black bread	το μαύρο ψωμί	to mávro psomí
bland	άνοστος	ánostos
blanket	η κουβέρτα	i koovérta
bleach	ξανθαίνω	xanthéno
blister	η φουσκάλα	i fooskála
blond	ξανθός	xanthós

blood	το αίμα	to éma
blood pressure	η αρτηριακή πίεση	i artiriakí píesi
blouse	η μπλούζα	i blóoza
blow-dry hair	στεγνώνω τα μαλλιά	steghnóno ta malyá
blue	μπλε	ble
boat	το καράβι	to karávi
body lotion	η λοσιόν	i losyón
body	το σώμα	to sóma
boiled	βρασμένος	vrazménos
bone	το κόκαλο	to kókalo
book	το βιβλίο	to vivlío
bookshop	το βιβλιοπωλείο	to vivliopolío
borders (of country)	τα σύνορα	ta sínora
bored, I am	βαριέμαι	varyéme
boring	πληκτικός	pliktikós
born	γεννημένος	yeniménos
borrow	δανείζομαι	dhanízome
boss	το αφεντικό	to afendikó
botanical gardens	ο βοτανικός κήπος	o votanikós kípos
both	και οι δύο/και τα δύο	ke i dhío/ke ta dhío
bothers me	μ' ενοχλεί	menochlí
bottle	το μπουκάλι	to bookáli
box (theater)	το θεωρείο	to theorío
box	το κουτί	to kootí
boy	το αγόρι	to aghóri
bra	το σουτιέν	to sootyén
bracelet	το βραχιόλι	to vrahyóli
braised	βρασμένος	vrazménos
brake	το φρένο	to fréno
brake fluid	το υγρό φρένου	to ighró frénoo
brake oil	το λάδι φρένου	to ládhi frénoo
brandy	το κονιάκ	to konyák
bread	το ψωμί	to psomí
break	σπάζω	spázo
breakfast	το πρωινό	to proinó
breast	στήθος	to stíthos
bridge	η γέφυρα	i yéfira
briefs	το σλιπάκι	to slipáki
bring	φέρνω	férno
brochure	το φυλλάδιο	to filádhyo
broken	σπασμένος, χαλασμένος	spazménos, chalazménos
broth	το ζουμί	to zoomí
brother	ο αδερφός	o adherfós
brown	καστανός	kastanós
brush	βούρτσα	i vóortsa
Brussels sprouts	η λαχανάκια Βρυξελλών	lachanákya vrixelón
bucket	ο κουβάς	o koovás
bugs	τα ζωύφια	ta zoífya
building	το κτίριο	to ktíryo
buoy	η σημαδούρα	i simadhóora
burglary	η διάρρηξη	i dhiárixi
burn	το έγκαυμα	to éngkavma
burn (verb)	καίω	kéo
burnt	καμένος	kaménos
bus stop	η στάση	i stási

15

bus station	το λεωφορείο λεωφορείων	o stathmós leoforíon
bus	ο σταθμός	to leoforío
business class	μπιζνεσκλάς	biznesklás
business trip	η περιοδεία	i perodhía
busy (phone)	κατειλημμένο	katiliméno
butane gas	το υγραέριο	to ighraério
butcher	ο χασάπης	o chasápis
butter	το βούτυρο	to vóotiro
button	το κουμπί	to koobí
buy	αγοράζω	aghorázo
by phone	τηλεφωνικώς	tilefonikós
by air	αεροπορικώς	aeroporikós

C

cabbage	το λάχανο	to láchano
cabin	η καμπίνα	i kabína
café	το καφενείο	to kafenío
cake	η πάστα, η τούρτα	i pásta, i tóorta
call (phone)	τηλεφωνώ	tilefonó
camera	η φωτογραφική μηχανή	i fotoghrafikí michaní
camp (verb)	κατασκηνώνω	kataskinóno
camp site	το κάμπινγκ	to kámping
camping	το κάμπιγκ	to kámping
camping guide	ο κατάλογος κατασκήνωσης	o katáloghos kataskínosis
camping permit	η άδεια κατασκήνωσης	i ádhya kataskínosis
camping shop	το μαγαζί του κάμπιγκ	to maghazí too kámping
camping van	το κάμπερ	to kámper
cancel	ακυρώνω	akiróno
candies	οι καραμέλες	i karaméles
candle	το κερί	to kerí
canned food	η κονσέρβα	i konsérva
canoe	το κανό	to kanó
canoe (verb)	κάνω κανό	káno kanó
car	το αυτοκίνητο	to aftokínito
car deck	το κατάστρωμα για τα αυτοκίνητα	to katástroma ya ta aftokínita
car papers	τα χαρτιά του αυτοκινήτου	ta chartyá too aftokinítoo
car park/parking space	το πάρκιγκ	to párking
car trouble	η βλάβη	i vlávi
carafe	η καράφα	i karáfa
cardigan	η ζακέτα	i zakéta
careful	προσεχτικός	prosechtikós
carriage (of train)	το βαγόνι	to vaghóni
carrot	το καρότο	to karóto
carton	η κούτα	i kóota
cashier	το ταμείο	to tamío
casino	το καζίνο	to kazíno
cassette/cartridge	η κασέτα	i kaséta
castle	το κάστρο	o kástro
cat	η γάτα	i gháta
catalog	ο κατάλογος	o katáloghos
cathedral	η μητρόπολη	i mitrópoli

cauliflower	το κουνουπίδι	to koonoopídhi
cave	η σπηλιά	i spilyá
celebrate	γιορτάζω	yortázo
celebration	η γιορτή	i yortí
cemetery	το νεκροταφείο	to nekrotafío
center	το κέντρο	to kéndro
centimeter	ο πόντος	o póndos
chain	η αλυσίδα	i alisídha
chair	η καρέκλα	i karékla
chalet area	ο χώρος με μπάγκαλοου	o chóros me bángaló-óo
chambermaid	η καμαριέρα	i kamaryéra
champagne	η σαμπάνια	i sampánya
change (verb)	αλλάζω	aláazo
change the oil	αλλάζω τα λάδια	aláazo ta ládhya
change (small)	τα ψιλά	ta psilá
change (baby's diaper)	καθαρίζω	katharízo
chapel	το εξωκλήσι	to exoklísi
charter flight	η πτήση τσάρτερ	i ptísi-tsárter
cheap	φτηνός	ftinós
check (verb)	ελέγχω	eléncho
check	η επιταγή	i epitayí
check in	τσεκάρω	tsekáro
checked luggage locker	η θυρίδα αποσκευών	i thirídha aposkevón
checked luggage office	ο χώρος αποσκευών	o chóros aposkevón
cheers	στην υγειά σας	stiniyásas
cheese	το τυρί	to tirí
cherries	τα κεράσια	ta kerásya
chess	το σκάκι	to skáki
chewing gum	η τσίχλα/η μαστίχα	i tsíchla/i mastícha
chicken	το κοτόπουλο	to kotópoolo
chicory	τα ραδίκια	ta radhíya
child	το παιδί	to pedhí
child seat (in car)	το παιδικό κάθισμα	to pedhikó káthizma
child seat (on bicycle)	η παιδική σέλα	i pedhikí séla
chin	το πηγούνι	to pighóoni
chocolate	η σοκολάτα	i sokoláta
choose	διαλέγω	dhialégho
christian/given name	το (μικρό) όνομα	to (mikró) ónoma
church	η εκκλησία	i eklisía
church service	η θεία λειτουργία	i thía litooryía
cigar	το πούρο	to póoro
cigarette paper	το τσιγαρόχαρτο	to tsigharócharto
cigarette	το τσιγάρο	to tsigháro
circle	ο κύκλος	o kíklos
circus	το τσίρκο	to tsírko
city	η πόλη	i póli
classical concert	η κλασσική συναυλία	i klasikí sinavlía
clean (verb)	καθαρίζω	katharízo
clean	καθαρός	katharós
clear (adj.)	σαφής	safís
clearance sale	το ξεπούλημα	to xepóolima
closed off	κλειστός	klistós
closed	κλειστός	klistós
clothes	τα ρούχα	ta róocha
clothesline	το σκοινί μπουγάδας	to skiní booghádhas
clothespin	το μανταλάκι	to mandaláki

clothes hanger	η κρεμάστρα	*i kremástra*
coach	το πούλμαν	*to póolman*
coat	το παλτό	*to paltó*
cobbler	ο τσαγκάρης	*o tsangáris*
cockroach	η κατσαρίδα	*i katsarídha*
cocoa (drink)	το γάλα με κακάο	*to ghála me kakáo*
cod (dried)	ο μπακαλιάρος	*o bakalyáros*
coffee	ο καφές	*o kafés*
cold (disease)	το κρυολόγημα	*to kriolóyima*
cold	κρύος	*kríos*
cold meats	τα αλλαντικά	*ta alandiká*
collarbone	το κλειδοκόκαλο	*to klidhokókalo*
colleague	ο συνάδερφος	*o sinádherfos*
collision	η σύγκρουση	*i síngroosi*
cologne	η κολόνια	*i kolónya*
color	το χρώμα	*to chróma*
color television	η έγχρωμη τηλεόραση	*i éngchromi tileórasi*
colored pencils	τα κραγιόνια	*ta krayónya*
comb	το χτένι	*to chténi*
come	έρχομαι	*érchome*
come back	ξαναέρχομαι	*xanaérchome*
compact disc	το κόμπακτ-ντισκ	*to kómpakt-disk*
compartment	το κουπέ	*to koopé*
complaint	το παράπονο	*to parápono*
complaints book	το βιβλίο παραπόνων	*to vivlío parapónon*
completely	τελείως	*telíos*
compliment	το κομπλιμέντο	*to kompliméndo*
compulsory	υποχρεωτικός	*ipochreotikós*
concert	η συναυλία	*i sinavlía*
concert hall	η αίθουσα συναυλιών	*i éthoosa sinavlyón*
concussion	η διάσειση εγκεφάλου	*i dhiásisi engkefáloo*
condom	το προφυλαχτικό	*to profilaktikó*
confectioner	ο ζαχαροπλάστης	*o zacharoplástis*
congratulate	συγχαίρω	*sinchéro*
connection	η ανταπόκριση	*i andapókrisi*
constipation	η δυσκοιλιότητα	*i dhiskilyótita*
consulate	το προξενείο	*to proxenío*
consultation	η επίσκεψη	*i epískepsi*
contact lens	ο φακός επαφής	*o fakós epafís*
contact lens solution	το υγρό για φακούς επαφής	*to ighró ya fakóos epafís*
contagious	κολλητικός	*kolitikós*
contraceptive	το αντισυλληπτικό	*to andisiliptikó*
contraceptive pill	το αντισυλληπτικό χάπι	*to andisiliptikó chápi*
cook	ο μάγειρας	*o máyiras*
cook (verb)	μαγειρεύω	*mayirévo*
copper/bronze	χάλκινος	*chálkinos*
copy	το αντίγραφο	*to andíghrafo*
corkscrew	το τιρμπουσόν	*to tirbooshón*
corner	η γωνιά	*i ghonyá*
cornflower	το κορν φλάουερ	*to kornfláwer*
correct	σωστός	*sostós*
correspond	αλληλογραφώ	*aliloghrafó*
corridor	ο διάδρομος	*o dhiádhromos*
cot	το παιδικό κρεβάτι	*to pedhikó kreváti*
cotton	το βαμβάκι	*to vamváki*
cotton (antiseptic)	το βαμβάκι	*to vamváki*

cough syrup	το σιρόπι για το βήχα	*to sirópi ya to vícha*
cough	ο βήχας	*o víchas*
counter	η θυρίδα	*i thirídha*
country	η χώρα	*i chóra*
country code	ο αριθμός της χώρας	*o arithmós tis chóras*
countryside	η εξοχή	*i exohí*
course of treatment	η θεραπεία	*i therapía*
cousin (female)	η ξαδέρφη	*i xadhérfi*
cousin (male)	ο ξάδερφος	*o xádherfos*
crab	ο κάβουρας	*o kávooras*
crackers	τα μπισκότα	*ta biskóta*
cream (ointment)	η κρέμα	*i kréma*
cream	το ανθόγαλα	*to anthóghala*
credit card	η πιστωτική κάρτα	*i pistotikí kárta*
cross the road	περνώ το δρόμο	*to dhrómo*
crossroads	το πέρασμα	*to pérazma*
cry (verb)	κλαίω	*kléo*
cubic meter	το κυβικό μέτρο	*to kivikó métro*
cucumber	το αγγούρι	*to anghóori*
cuff links	τα μανικετόκουμπα	*ta maniketókooma*
cup	το φλιτζάνι	*to flidzáni*
curly	σγουρός	*zghoorós*
current (water)	το ρεύμα	*to révma*
current (electricity)	το ρεύμα	*to révma*
cushion	το μαξιλαράκι	*to maxilaráki*
custard	η κρέμα	*i kréma*
customary	συνηθισμένος	*sinithizménos*
customs	το τελωνείο	*to telonío*
customs officer	ο τελώνης	*o telónis*
customs check	ο τελωνιακός έλεγχος	*o teloniakós élenchos*
cut (verb)	κόβω	*kóvo*
cutlery	τα μαχαιροπήρουνα	*ta maheropíroona*
cyclist	ο ποδηλάτης	*o podhilátis*

D
damage	η βλάβη	*i vlávi*
dance (verb)	χορεύω	*chorévo*
dandruff	η πιτυρίδα	*i pitirídha*
danger	ο κίνδυνος	*o kíndhinos*
dangerous	επικίνδυνος	*epikíndhinos*
dark	σκοτεινός	*skotinós*
daughter	η κόρη	*i kóri*
day after tomorrow	μεθαύριο	*methávrio*
day	η μέρα	*i méra*
day (24 hours)	το μερόνυχτο	*to merónichto*
day before yesterday	προχτές	*prochtés*
dead	νεκρός	*nekrós*
decaffeinated	χωρίς καφείνη	*chorís kafeíni*
December	ο Δεκέμβριος	*o dekémvrios*
deck chair	η ξαπλώστρα, η σαιζ-λόνγκ	*i xaplóstra, i sezlóng*
declare (customs)	δηλώνω	*dhilóno*
deep	βαθύς	*vathís*
deep frozen	καταψυγμένος	*katapsighménos*
deep sea diving	η κατάδυση σε μεγάλο βάθος	*i katádhisi se meghálo váthos*
defective	ελαττωματικός	*elatomatikós*

degrees	οι βαθμοί	i vathmí
delay (noun)	η καθυστέρηση	i kathistérisi
delicious	εξαιρετικός	exeretikós
dentist	ο οδοντογιατρός	o odhondoyatrós
dentures	η μασέλα	maséla
deodorant	το αποσμητικό	to apozmitikó
department (in store)	το τμήμα	to tmíma
department store	ο εμπορικός οίκος	o emborikós íkos
departure	η αναχώρηση	i anachórisi
departure time	η ώρα αναχώρησης	i óra anachórisis
depilatory cream	το αποτριχωτικό	to apotrichotikó
deposit	η εγγύηση	i engíisi
dessert	το επιδόρπιο	to epidhórpyo
destination	ο προορισμός	o pro-orizmós
details (personal etc.)	τα στοιχεία	ta stihía
detergent	το απορρυπαντικό	to aporipandikó
develop (film)	εμφανίζω	emfanízo
diabetic	ο διαβητικός	o dhiavitikós
dial	παίρνω	pérno
diamond	το διαμάντι	to dhiamándi
diaper	η πάνα	i pána
diarrhea	η διάρροια	i dhiária
dictionary	το λεξικό	to lexikó
diesel oil	το (λάδι)	to (ládhi) dízel
diet	η δίαιτα	i dhíeta
difficulty	η δυσκολία	i dhiskolía
dine	δειπνώ	dhipnó
dining car	το βαγόνι-εστιατόριο	to vaghóni-estiatório
dining room	η τραπεζαρία	i trapezaría
dinner	το δείπνο	to dhípno
dinner jacket	το σμόκιν	to smókin
direction	η κατεύθυνση	i katéfthinsi
directly	κατ' ευθείαν	katefthían
dirty	βρόμικος	vrómikos
disabled	ανάπηρος	anápiros
disco	η ντίσκο	i dísko
discount	η έκπτωση	i ékptosi
dish of the day	το πιάτο της ημέρας	to pyáto tis iméras
disinfectant	το απολυμαντικό	to apolimandikó
displeased, I am	μου κακοφαίνεται	moo kakofénete
distance	η απόσταση	i apóstasi
distilled water	το διυλισμένο νερό	to dhiilizméno neró
disturb	ενοχλώ	enochló
disturbance	η διατάραξη	i dhiatáraxi
dive	βουτώ	vootó
diving	η κατάδυση	i katádhisi
diving board	ο βατήρας	o vatíras
diving gear	τα εξαρτήματα κατάδυσης	ta exartímata katádhisis
divorced	χωρισμένος	chorizménos
dizzy	ζαλισμένος	zalizménos
do	κάνω	káno
do night duty	διανυκτερεύω	dhianikterévo
doctor	ο γιατρός	o yatrós
dog	ο σκύλος	o skílos
doll	η κούκλα	o kóokla
domestic (e.g. flights)	εσωτερικός	esoterikós

door	η πόρτα	i pórta
double/for two	για δύο άτομα	ya dhío átoma
down	κάτω	káto
drachma	η δραχμή	i dhrachmí
draft, there's a	κάνει ρεύμα	káni révma
dream	ονειρεύομαι	onirévome
dress	το φόρεμα	to fórema
dressing gown	η ρόμπα	i róba
dried fruit	ξηροί καρποί	xirí karpí
drink (verb)	πίνω	píno
drink	το ποτό	to potó
drinking water	το πόσιμο νερό	to pósimo neró
drive	οδηγώ	odhighó
driver	ο οδηγός	o odhighós
driving license	η άδεια οδηγήσεως	i ádhya odhiyíseos
drought	η ξηρασία	i xirasía
dry clean	στεγνοκαθαρίζω	steghnokatharízo
dry cleaner	το στεγνοκαθαριστήριο	to steghnokatharistírio
dry (verb)	στεγνώνω	steghnóno
dry	ξηρός	xirós
dry shampoo	το στεγνό σαμπουάν	to steghnó sampwán
during the day	την ημέρα	tin iméra
during	κατά την διάρκεια	katá ti dhiarkía

E

ear	το αυτί	to avtí
ear, nose and throat specialist	ο ωτορινολαρυγγολόγος	o otorinolaringhológhos
eardrops	οι σταγόνες για τα αυτιά	i staghónes ya ta aftyá
early	νωρίς	norís
earrings	τα σκουλαρίκια	ta skoolaríkya
earth	το χώμα	to chóma
earthenware	η κεραμική	i keramikí
east	η ανατολή	i anatolí
easy	εύκολος	éfkolos
eat	τρώω	tró-o
eczema	το έκζεμα	to ékzema
eel	το χέλι	to héli
egg	το αυγό	to avghó
eggplant	η μελιτζάνα	i melitzána
electric	ηλεκτρικός	ilektrikós
electrical connection	η ηλεκτρική σύνδεση	i ilektrikí síndhesi
elevator	το ασανσέρ/ο ανελκυστήρας	to asansér/o anelkistíras
embassy	η πρεσβεία	i prezvía
emergency exit	η έξοδος κινδύνου	i éxodhos kindhínoo
emergency number	ο αριθμός του συναγερμού	o arithmós too sinayermóo
emergency signal	το σήμα κινδύνου	to síma kindhínoo
emergency triangle/cone	το τρίγωνο κινδύνου	to tríghono kindhínoo
empty	άδειος	ádhyos
England	η Αγγλία	i anglía
English	τα αγγλικά	ta angliká
enjoy	απολαμβάνω	apolamváno
entertainment	η διασκέδαση	i dhiaskédhasi

15

entertainment guide (Athens only)	το Αθηνόραμα	to athinórama
entrance	η είσοδος	i ísodhos
envelope	ο φάκελος	o fákelos
environment	το περιβάλλον	to periválon
escort	η/ο συνοδός	io sinodhós
essentially	ουσιαστικά	oosiastiká
evening	το βράδυ	to vrádhi
evening dress	η βραδινή ενδυμασία	i vradhiní endhimasía
evening meal	το δείπνο	to dhípno
event	το γεγονός	to yeghonós
every time	κάθε φορά	káthe forá
everything	τα πάντα	ta pánda
everywhere	παντού	pandóo
examine	εξετάζω	exetázo
excavations	οι ανασκαφές	i anaskafés
excellent	υπέροχος	ipérochos
exchange (money)	αλλάζω	aláxo
exchange	ανταλλάσσω	antaláso
exchange office	το γραφείο συναλλάγματος	to ghrafío sinalághmatos
excursion	η εκδρομή	i ekdhromí
exhibition	η έκθεση	i ékthesi
exit	η έξοδος	i éxodhos
expenses	τα έξοδα	ta éxodha
expensive	ακριβός	akrivós
explain	εξηγώ	exighó
express train	η ταχεία	i tahía
external	εξωτερικός	exoterikós
eye	το μάτι	to máti
eye specialist	ο οφθαλμίατρος	o ofthalmíatros
eyedrops	οι σταγόνες για τα μάτια	i staghónes ya ta mátya
eyeliner	το μολύβι για τα μάτια	to molívi ya ta mátya

F

face	το πρόσωπο	to prósopo
factory	το εργοστάσιο	to erghostásyo
fall	πέφτω	péfto
family	η οικογένεια	i ikoyénya
famous	ξακουστός	xakoostós
far away	μακριά	makriá
farm	το αγρόκτημα	to aghróktima
farmer	ο γεωργός	o yeorghós
fashion	η μόδα	i módha
father	ο πατέρας	o patéras
fax (verb)	στέλνω ένα φαξ	stélno éna fax
February	ο Φεβρουάριος	o fevrooários
feel like	έχω διάθεση	écho dhiáthesi
feel like	αισθάνομαι	esthánome
ferry	το φέρρυ-μπωτ	to féribot
festival	η γιορτή	i yortí
fever	ο πυρετός	o piretós
fill (tooth)	σφραγίζω	sfrayízo
fill/top up	γεμίζω	yemízo

fill out	συμπληρώνω	*simpliróno*
filling	το σφράγισμα	*to sfráyizma*
film	η ταινία	*i tenía*
film (camera)	το φιλμ	*to film*
filter	το φίλτρο	*to fíltro*
find	βρίσκω	*vrísko*
fine	η κλήση	*i klísi*
finger	το δάχτυλο	*to dháchtilo*
fingernail	το νύχι	*to níhi*
fire	η φωτιά	*i fotyá*
fire (accidental)	η πυρκαγιά	*i pirkayá*
fire department	η πυροσβεστική υπηρεσία	*i pirosvestikí ipiresía*
fire escape	η σκάλα πυρκαγιάς	*i skála pirkayás*
fire extinguisher	ο πυροσβεστήρας	*o pirosvestíras*
first	πρώτος	*prótos*
first aid	οι πρώτες βόηθειες	*i prótes voíthyes*
first class	η πρώτη θέση	*i próti thési*
fish (verb)	ψαρεύω	*psarévo*
fish	το ψάρι	*to psári*
fishing rod	το αγκίστρι	*to angístri*
fitness club	το γυμναστήριο	*to yimnastírio*
fitting room	το δοκιμαστήριο	*to dhokimastíryo*
fix	φτιάχνω	*ftyáchno*
flag	η σημαία	*i siméa*
flash bulb	η λάμπα φλας	*i lámpa flash*
flash cubes	οι λάμπες φλας	*i lámpes flash*
flash gun	το φλας	*to flash*
flea market	το παλιατζίδικο	*to paliatzídhiko*
flight	η πτήση	*i ptísi*
flight number	ο αριθμός της πτήσης	*o arithmós tis ptísis*
flood	η πλημμύρα	*i plimíra*
floor	ο όροφος	*o órofos*
flour	το αλεύρι	*to alévri*
flu	η γρίπη	*i ghrípi*
fly	η μύγα	*i mígha*
fly (verb)	πετώ	*petó*
foggy, it is	έχει ομίχλη	*éhi omíchli*
folding trailer	το λυόμενο τροχόσπιτο	*to liómeno trochóspito*
folkloristic	λαογραφικός	*laoghrafikós*
follow	ακολουθώ	*akoloothó*
food	το φαγητό	*to fayitó*
food	τα τρόφιμα	*ta trófima*
food poisoning	η τροφική δηλητηρίαση	*i trofikí dhilitiríasi*
foot	το πόδι	*to pódhi*
for hire	ενοικιάζεται	*nikyázete*
forbidden, it is	απαγορεύεται	*apaghorévete*
forehead	το μέτωπο	*to métopo*
foreign	εξωτερικός	*exoterikós*
forget	ξεχνάω	*xechnáo*
fork	το πηρούνι	*to piróoni*
form	το έντυπο	*to éndipo*
fort	το κάστρο	*to kástro*
fountain	το συντριβάνι	*to sindriváni*
frame	ο σκελετός	*o skeletós*
free	ελεύθερος	*eléftheros*
free (of charge)	δωρεάν	*dhoreán*

free time	η ελεύθερη ώρα	*i eléftheri óra*
freeze	παγώνω	*paghóno*
French	τα γαλλικά	*ta ghaliká*
French bread	το ψωμί μπαστούνι	*to psomí bastóoni*
French fries	πατάτες τηγανιτές	*patátes tighanités*
fresh	φρέσκος	*fréskos*
Friday	η Παρασκευή	*i paraskeví*
fried	τηγανητός	*tighanitós*
fried egg	το αυγό μάτι	*to avghó máti*
friend	ο φίλος	*o fílos*
friendly	ευγενικός	*evyenikós*
fritter	η τηγανίτα	*i tighaníta*
front, at the	μπροστά	*brostá*
frozen	καταψυγμένος	*katapsighménos*
fruit	το φρούτο	*to fróoto*
fruit juice	ο χυμός	*o chimós*
frying pan	το τηγάνι	*to tigháni*
full	γεμάτος	*yemátos*

G

gallery (theater)	ο εξώστης	*o exóstis*
game	το παιχνίδι	*to pechnídi*
garage	το γκαράζ	*to garáz*
garbage bag	η σακούλα σκουπιδιών	*sakóola skoopidhyón*
garden	ο κήπος	*o kípos*
gas (high octane)	η σούπερ	*i sóoper*
gas station	το βενζινάδικο	*venzinádhiko*
gasoline	η βενζίνη	*i venzíni*
gauze	η γάζα	*i gháza*
gear	η ταχύτητα	*i tahítita*
gel	το τζελ	*to dzel*
gentleman	ο κύριος	*o kírios*
German	τα γερμανικά	*ta yermaniká*
get lost	χάνω το δρόμο	*cháno to dhrómo*
get off/out	κατεβαίνω	*katevéno*
gift	το δώρο	*to dhóro*
girl	το κορίτσι	*to korítsi*
girlfriend	η φίλη	*i fíli*
giro card	η ταχυδρομική κάρτα	*i tahidhromikí kárta*
giro check	η ταχυδρομική επιταγή	*i tahidhromikí epitayí*
glass	το ποτήρι	*to potíri*
glasses (sun-, reading-)	τα γυαλιά	*ta yalyá*
gliding	η ανεμοπορία	*i anemoporía*
glove	το γάντι	*to ghándi*
glue	η κόλλα	*i kóla*
go	πηγαίνω	*piyéno*
go back	γυρίζω	*yirízo*
go out	βγαίνω έξω	*vyéno éxo*
goat's cheese	το κατσικίσιο τυρί	*to katsikísyo tirí*
gold	το χρυσάφι	*to chrisáfi*
gold-plated	επίχρυσος	*epíchrisos*
golf	το γκολφ	*to golf*
golf coarse	το γήπεδο του γκολφ	*to yípedho too golf*
good afternoon	καλημέρα	*kaliméra*
good day	καλημέρα	*kaliméra*
good evening	καλησπέρα	*kalispéra*
good luck	η ευτυχία	*i eftihía*

Word list

15

good morning	καλημέρα	*kaliméra*
good night	καληνύχτα	*kaliníchta*
good-bye	γειά σας, γειά σου	*yásas, yáso*
good-bye (farewell)	ο αποχαιρετισμός	*o apoheretizmós*
grade crossing	η διάβαση	*i dhiávasi*
gram	το γραμμάριο	*to ghramário*
grandchild	το εγγόνι	*to engóni*
grandfather	ο παππούς	*o papóos*
grandmother	η γιαγιά	*i yayá*
grape juice	ο χυμός σταφυλιών	*o chimós stafilyón*
grapefruit	η φράπα	*i frápa*
grapes	τα σταφύλια	*ta stafílya*
grave	ο τάφος	*o táfos*
gray	γκρίζος	*grízos*
grease	τα λίπη	*ta lípi*
green	πράσινος	*prásinos*
green card	η πράσινη κάρτα	*i prásini kárta*
greet	χαιρετίζω	*heretízo*
greetings	τα χαιρετίσματα	*ta heretízmata*
grill (verb)	ψήνω στα κάρβουνα	*psíno sta kárvoona*
grilled	ψητός	*psitós*
grocer	ο μπακάλης	*o bakális*
ground	το χώμα	*to chóma*
ground meat	ο κιμάς	*o kimás*
group	το γκρουπ	*to groop*
guest house	η πανσιόν	*i pansyón*
guide (person)	ο ξεναγός	*o xenaghós*
guidebook	ο οδηγός	*o odhighós*
guided tour	η ξενάγηση	*i xenáyisi*
guilt	η ενοχή	*i enohí*
gynecologist	ο γυναικολόγος	*o yinekológhos*

H

hair	τα μαλλιά	*ta malyá*
hair cream	το βερνίκι για τα μαλλιά	*to verníki ya ta malyá*
hairdresser	ο κομμωτής	*o komotís*
hairpins	οι καρφίτσες	*i karfítses*
half	μισό	*misó*
half kilo	το μισό κιλό	*to misó kiló*
half-full	μισογεμάτος	*misoyemátos*
ham	το ζαμπόν	*to zambón*
hammer	το σφυρί	*to sfirí*
hand brake	το χειρόφρενο	*to hirófreno*
hand	το χέρι	*to héri*
handbag	η τσάντα	*i tsánda*
handmade	χειροποίητος	*hiropíitos*
handicraft	η χειροτεχνία	*i hirotechnía*
handkerchief	το μαντήλι	*to mandíli*
handsome	ωραίος	*oréos*
happy	χαρούμενος	*charóomenos*
harbor	το λιμάνι	*to limáni*
hard	σκληρός	*sklirós*
hat	το καπέλο	*to kapélo*
hayfever	ο αλλεργικός κατάρρους	*o aleryikós katároos*
hazelnut	το φουντούκι	*to foondóoki*

head	το κεφάλι	to kefáli
headache	ο πονοκέφαλος	o ponokéfalos
health	η υγεία	i iyía
heart	η καρδιά	i kardhyá
heart patient	ο καρδιακός	o kardhiakós
heater	το καλοριφέρ	to kalorifér
heavy	βαρύς	varís
hedge	ο φράχτης	o fráchtis
heel (of shoe)	το τακούνι	to takóoni
hello	γειά σας, γειά σου	yásas, yásoo
helmet	το κράνος	to krános
help	η βοήθεια	i voíthya
help (verb)	βοηθώ	voithó
herb tea	το τσάι του βουνού	to tsái too voonóo
herbs	τα μπαχαρικά	ta bachar!ká
here	εδώ	edhó
herring (smoked)	η ρέγγα	rénga
high	ψηλός	psilós
high tide	η παλίρροια	i palíria
highchair	η παιδική καρέκλα	i pedhikí karékla
highway	η εθνική οδός	i ethnikí odhós
hiking	η πεζοπορία	i pezoporía
hiking (alpine)	η ορειβασία	i orivasía
hiking boots	τα παπούτσια ορειβασίας	ta papóotsya orivasías
hip	ο γοφός	o ghofós
hire	νοικιάζω	nikyázo
hitchhiking	το ωτοστόπ	to otostóp
hobby	το χόμπυ	to chóbi
hold-up	η επίθεση	i epíthesi
holiday rental	το εξοχικό σπιτάκι	to exohikó spitáki
holiday (public)	η γιορτή	i yortí
holidays	οι διακοπές	i dhiakopés
homesickness	η νοσταλγία	i nostalyía
honest	τίμιος	tímyos
honey	το μέλι	to méli
hood (car)	το καπό	to kapó
horizontal	οριζόντιος	orizóndios
horrible	απαίσιος	apésios
horse	το άλογο	to álogho
hospital	το νοσοκομείο	to nosokomío
hospitality	η φιλοξενία	i filoxenía
hot	ζεστός	zestós
hot (spicy)	πικάντικος	pikándikos
hot spring	η θερμική πηγή	i thermikí piyí
hotwater bottle	η θερμοφόρα	i thermofóra
hotel	το ξενοδοχείο	to xenodhohío
hour	η ώρα	i óra
house	το σπίτι	to spíti
household items	τα οικιακά αντικείμενα	ta ikyaká andikímena
housewife	η νοικοκυρά	i nikokirá
how	πώς;	pos?
how far?	πόσο μακρυά;	póso makriá?
how long?	πόσο καιρό;	póso kyeró?
how much?	πόσο;	póso?
hundred grams	εκατό γραμμάρια	ekató ghramárya
hunger	η πείνα	i pína

hurricane	ο τυφώνας	o tifónas
hurry (be in a)	βιάζομαι	vyázome
husband	ο σύζυγος	o sízighos
hut	η καλύβα	i kalíva
hyperventilation	η υπεροξυγόνωση	i iperoxighónosi

I

ice	ο πάγος	o pághos
ice cream	το παγωτό	to paghotó
ice cubes	τα παγάκια	ta paghákya
idea	η ιδέα	i idhéa
identification	η ταυτότητα	i taftótita
identify	αναγνωρίζω	anaghnorízo
ignition key	το κλειδί επαφής	to klidhí epafís
illness	η αρρώστια	i aróstia
illustrated book	το εικονογραφημένο βιβλίο	to ikonoghrafiméno vivlío
imagine	φαντάζομαι	fandázome
immediately	αμέσως	amésos
import duty	τα εισαγωγικά τέλη	ta isaghoyiká téli
impossible	αδύνατος	adhínatos
in	σε	se
in front	μπροστά	brostá
in front of	μπροστά σε	brostá se
in safe-keeping	σε φύλαξη	se fílaxi
in the evening/at night	το βράδυ	to vrádhi
included (it is)	συμπεριλαμβάνεται	simperilamvánete
indicate	δείχνω	dhíchno
indicator	το φλας	to flash
indigestion	η δυσπεψία	i dhispepsía
inflammation	η φλεγμονή	i fleghmoní
information office	το γραφείο πληροφοριών	to ghrafío pliroforyón
information	οι πληροφορίες	i plirofóries
information (piece of)	η πληροφορία	i pliroforía
injection	η ένεση	i énesi
injured	λαβωμένος	lavoménos
inner tube	το εσωτερικό λάστιχο	to esoterikó lásticho
innocent	αθώος	athóos
insect	το έντομο	to éndomo
insect repellent	λάδι για τα κουνούπια	ládhi ya ta koonóopya
insect bite	το τσίμπημα εντόμου	to tsímbima endómoo
inside	μέσα	mésa
insole	η εσωτερική σόλα	i esoterikí sóla
instructions for use	οι οδηγίες χρήσεως	i odhiyíes chríseos
insurance	η ασφάλεια	i asfálya
internal	εσωτερικός	esoterikós
international	διεθνής	dhiethnís
interpreter	ο διερμηνέας	o dhierminéas
intersection	η διασταύρωση	i dhiastávrosi
interval	το διάλειμμα	to dhiálima
introduce	γνωρίζω	ghnorízo
introduce myself	συστήνομαι	sistínome
invite	προσκαλώ	proskaló
iodine	το ιώδιο	to iódhio
Ireland	η Ιρλανδία	i irlandhía
iron	το σίδερο	to sídhero

Word list

15

iron (verb)	σιδερώνω	*sidheróno*
ironing board	η σανίδα σιδερώματος	*i sanídha sidherómatos*
island	το νησί	*to nisí*
Italian	τα ιταλικά	*ta italiká*
itch	η φαγούρα	*i faghóora*
item of clothing	το ρούχο	*to róocho*
itinerary	το δρομολόγιο	*to dhromolóyo*

J

jack	ο γρύλλος	*o ghrílos*
jacket	η ζακέτα	*i zakéta*
jam	η μαρμελάδα	*i marmeládha*
January	ο Ιανουάριος	*o yanooários*
jaw	το σαγόνι	*to saghóni*
jellyfish	η μέδουσα	*i médhoosa*
jeweler	ο χρυσοχόος	*o chrisochóos*
jewelery	τα κοσμήματα	*ta kozmímata*
jog (running)	το τρέξιμο	*to tréximo*
joke	το αστείο	*to astío*
juice	ο χυμός	*o himós*
July	ο Ιούλιος	*o yóolios*
jumper cables	το καλώδιο εκκίνησης	*to kalódhio ekkínisis*
June	ο Ιούνιος	*o yóonios*
junk shop	το παλιατζίδικο	*to paliadzídhiko*

K

kettle	ο βραστήρας	*o vrastíras*
key	το κλειδί	*to klidhí*
kilo	το κιλό	*to kiló*
kilometer	το χιλιόμετρο	*to hilyómetro*
king	ο βασιλιάς	*o vasilyás*
kiosk	το περίπτερο	*to períptero*
kiss	το φιλί	*to filí*
kiss (verb)	φιλώ	*filó*
kitchen	η κουζίνα	*i koozína*
knee	το γόνατο	*to ghónato*
knife	το μαχαίρι	*to machéri*
knit	πλέκω	*pléko*
know (person)	γνωρίζω	*ghnorízo*
know	ξέρω	*xéro*

L

lace	η δαντέλα	*i dhantéla*
ladies' room	η τουαλέτα γυναικών	*i twaléta yinekón*
lady	η κυρία	*i kiría*
lake	η λίμνη	*i límni*
lamb chop	το παϊδάκι	*to paidháki*
lamp	η λάμπα	*i lámpa*
land (verb)	προσγειώνομαι	*prosyiónome*
lane (on road)	η λωρίδα	*i lorídha*
language	η γλώσσα	*i ghlóssa*
lard	το λαρδί	*to lardhí*
large	μεγάλος	*meghálos*
last	τελευταίος	*teleftéos*
last night	χθες τη νύχτα	*chthes ti níchta*
late	αργά	*arghá*
latest, at the	το αργότερο	*to arghótero*

laugh	γελάω	yeláo
launderette	το πλυντήριο	to plindírio
lavatory	η τουαλέτα	i twaléta
law (studies)	τα νομικά	ta nomiká
lawyer	ο δικηγόρος	o dhikighóros
laxative	το καθαρτικό	to kathartikó
leaking	τρυπημένος	tripiménos
leather	το δέρμα	to dhérma
leather goods	τα δερμάτινα είδη	ta dhermátina ídhi
leave (verb)	φεύγω	févgho
leek	το πράσο	to práso
left (adj.)	αριστερός	aristerós
left (on/to the)	αριστερά	aristerá
leg	το πόδι	to pódhi
lemon	το λεμόνι	to lemóni
lemonade	η λεμονάδα	i lemonádha
lens	ο φακός	o fakós
lentils	οι φακές	i fakés
less	λιγότερο	lighótero
lesson	το μάθημα	to máthima
letter	το γράμμα	to ghrámma
lettuce	το μαρούλι	to maróoli
library	η βιβλιοθήκη	i vivliothíki
lie	λέω ψέματα	léo psémata
lie down	ξαπλώνομαι	xaplónome
lifeguard	ο ακτοφύλακας	o aktofílakas
light	το φως	o fos
light (color)	ανοιχτός	anichtós
light (weight)	ελαφρός	elafrós
lighter	ο αναπτήρας	o anaptíras
lighthouse	ο φάρος	o fáros
lightning	ο κεραυνός	o keravnós
like, I	μ' αρέσει	marési
line	η γραμμή	i ghramí
linen	το λινό	to linó
liquor store	η κάβα	i káva
lipstick	το κραγιόν	to krayón
listen	ακούω	akóo-o
liter	το λίτρο	to lítro
literature	η λογοτεχνία	i loghotechnía
little	λίγος	líghos
live	μένω	méno
live together	συγκατοικώ	singkatikó
lively	ζωηρός	zoirós
lobster	ο αστακός	o astakós
local	τοπικός	topikós
local (area) code	ο κωδικός της πόλης	o kodhikós tis pólis
lock	η κλειδαριά	i klidharyá
long (tall)	μακρύς	makrís
long (of time)	πολύς	polís
long distance call	υπεραστικός	iperastikós
look	κοιτάζω	kitázo
lose	χάνω	cháno
loss	ο χαμός, η απώλεια	o chamós, i apólya
lost and found	τα ευρεθέντα αντικείμενα	ta evrethénda andikímena
lost	χαμένος	chaménos

lotion	η λοσιόν	i losión
loud	δυνατά	dhinatá
love (verb)	αγαπώ	aghapó
love	η αγάπη	i aghápi
love with, be in	είμαι ερωτευμένος με	íme erotevménos me
low	χαμηλός	chamilós
low tide	η άμπωτη	i ámboti
luggage	οι αποσκευές	i aposkevés
luggage locker	η θυρίδα αποσκευών	i thirídha aposkevón
lunch	το γεύμα	to yévma
lungs	οι πνεύμονες	i pnévmones

M

machine	η μηχανή	i michaní
magazine	το περιοδικό	to periodhikó
mail	το ταχυδρομείο	to tahidhromío
mailbox	το γραμματοκιβώτιο	to ghramatokivótyo
mailman	ο ταχυδρόμος	o tahidhrómos
main road	ο μεγάλος δρόμος	o meghálos dhrómos
main post office	το κεντρικό ταχυδρομείο	to kendrikó tahidhromío
make an appointment/ a date	δίνω ραντεβού	dhíno randevóo
make love	κάνω έρωτα	káno érota
man	ο άντρας	o ándras
manager	ο διαχειριστής	o dhiahiristís
mandarin (orange)	το μανταρίνι	to mandaríni
manicure	το μανικιούρ	to manikyóor
map	ο χάρτης	o chártis
marble	το μάρμαρο	to mármaro
March	ο Μάρτιος	o mártis
margarine	η μαργαρίνη	i margharíni
marina	η μαρίνα	i marína
market	η αγορά	i aghorá
marriage	ο γάμος	o ghámos
married	παντρεμένος	pandreménos
married, get	παντρεύομαι	pandrévome
massage	το μασάζ	to masáz
match	ο αγώνας	o aghónas
matches	τα σπίρτα	ta spírta
matte (photographs)	ματ	mat
May	Ο Μάιος	o máios
maybe	ίσως	ísos
mayonnaise	η μαγιονέζα	i mayionéza
mayor	ο δήμαρχος	o dhímarchos
meal	το γεύμα	to yévma
mean	σημαίνω	siméno
means	το μέσο	to méso
meat	το κρέας	to kréas
medication	το φάρμακο	to fármako
medicine (liquid)	το σιρόπι	to sirópi
medicine	το φάρμακο	to fármako
melon	το πεπόνι	to pepóni
membership	η ιδιότητα του μέλους	i idhiótita too méloos
menstruate	έχω περίοδο	écho períodho
menstruation	η περίοδος	i períodhos
menu	το μενού, ο κατάλογος	to menóo o katáloghos

menu of the day	το μενού της ημέρας	to menóo tis iméras
message	η παραγγελία	i parangelía
metal	το μέταλλο	to métalo
meter	ο μετρητής	o metritís
meter	το μέτρο	to métro
middle, in the	στη μέση	sti mési
migraine	η ημικρανία	i imikranía
mild (tobacco)	ελαφρός	elafrós
milk	το γάλα	to ghála
milk products	τα προϊόντα γάλακτος	ta proiónda ghálaktos
milk for coffee	το γάλα για τον καφέ	to ghála ya tongafé
millimeter	το χιλιοστόμετρο	to hilyostómetro
mineral water	το μεταλλικό νερό	to metalikó neró
minute	το λεπτό	to leptó
mirror	ο καθρέφτης	o kathréftis
miss (I)	μου λείπει	moo lípi
missing (is)	λείπει	lípi
missing (person)	χαμένος	chaménos
mist	η ομίχλη	i omíchli
mistake	το λάθος	to láthos
mistaken, be	κάνω λάθος	káno láthos
Mister	ο κύριος	o kírios
misunderstanding	η παρεξήγηση	i parexíyisi
mocha	η μόκα	i móka
modern art	η σύγχρονη τέχνη	i sínghroni téchni
molar	ο τραπεζίτης	o trapezítis
moment	η στιγμή	i stighmí
monastery	το μοναστήρι	to monastíri
Monday	η Δευτέρα	i deftéra
money	τα λεφτά	ta leftá
month	ο μήνας	o mínas
moped	το μηχανάκι	to michanáki
morning (in the)	το πρωί	to proí
morning-after-pill	το μόρνιγκ-άφτερ-χάπι	to mórning-áfter-chápi
mosque	το τζαμί	to dzamí
mosquito	το κουνούπι	to koonóopi
motel	το μοτέλ	to motél
mother	η μητέρα	i mitéra
motorboat	η βενζινάκατος	i venzinákatos
motorcycle	η μοτοσικλέτα	i motosikléta
mountain hut	το ορειβατικό καταφύγιο	to orivatikó katafíyo
mountain	το βουνό	to voonó
mouse	το ποντίκι	to pondíki
mouth	το στόμα	to stóma
move back	κάνω πίσω	káno píso
Mrs.	η κυρία	i kiría
much/many	πολύς	polís
multistory car park	το σκεπασμένο πάρκιγκ	to skepazméno párking
muscle	ο μυς	o mis
muscle spasm	ο σπασμός	o spazmós
museum	το μουσείο	to moosío
mushrooms	τα μανιτάρια	ta manitárya
music	η μουσική	i moosikí
musical (show)	η μουσική κωμωδία	i moosikí komodhía

mussels	τα μύδια	*ta mídhya*
mustard	η μουστάρδα	*i moostárdha*
my name is	λέγομαι/με λένε	*léghome/me léne*

N

nail	το καρφί	*to karfí*
nail file	η λίμα για τα νύχια	*i líma ya ta níhya*
nail polish remover	το ασετόν	*to asetón*
nail polish	το βερνίκι νυχιών	*to verníki nihyón*
nail scissors	το ψαλιδάκι για τα νύχια	*to psalidháki yia ta níhya*
naked	γυμνός	*yimnós*
napkin	η πετσέτα	*i petséta*
National Health Office	το ταμείο ασθενείας	*to tamío asthenías*
nationality	η υπηκοότητα	*i ipikoótita*
naturally	φυσικά	*fisiká*
nature	η φύση	*i físi*
nauseous, I feel	ανακατεύεται το στομάχι μου	*anakatévete to stomáchi moo*
near	κοντά	*kondá*
near to	κοντά σε	*kondá se*
necessary	αναγκαίος	*anangéos*
neck	ο σβέρκος	*o zvérkos*
nectarine	το νεκταρίνι	*to nektaríni*
needle	το βελόνι	*to velóni*
negative	το αρνητικό	*to arnitikó*
neighbors	οι γείτονες	*i yítones*
nephew	ο ανιψιός	*o anipsyós*
never	ποτέ	*poté*
new	καινούριος	*kenóorios*
news	τα νέα	*ta néa*
newspaper	η εφημερίδα	*i efimerídha*
next	επόμενος	*epómenos*
next to	δίπλα σε	*dhípla se*
nice-looking	ωραίος	*oréos*
nice (people, things and events)	καλός	*kalós*
niece	η ανιψιά	*i anipsyá*
night life	η νυχτερινή ζωή	*i nichteriní zoí*
night	το βράδυ	*to vrádhi*
night	η νύχτα	*i níchta*
nightclub	το νυχτερινό κέντρο	*to nichterinó kéndro*
no	όχι	*óhi*
no one	κανένας	*kanénas*
no passing	απαγορεύεται η προσπέραση	*apaghorévete i prospérasi*
noise	ο θόρυβος	*o thórivos*
non-stop	χωρίς σταθμούς	*chorís stathmóos*
nonsense	οι σαχλαμάρες	*i sachlamáres*
normal	κανονικός	*kanonikós*
north	ο βοριάς	*o voryás*
nose	η μύτη	*i míti*
nose drops	οι σταγόνες για τη μύτη	*i staghónes ya ti míti*
nosebleed	η ρινορραγία	*i rinoragía*
notepaper	το χαρτί της αλληλογραφίας	*to chartí aliloghrafías*

nothing	τίποτα	*típota*
November	ο Νοέμβριος	*o noémvrios*
nowhere	πουθενά	*poothená*
nude	γυμνός	*yimnós*
nudism	ο γυμνισμός	*o yimnizmós*
nudist beach	η πλαζ για γυμνιστές	*i plaz ya yimnistés*
number	ο αριθμός	*o arithmós*
number plate	ο αριθμός κυκλοφορίας	*o arithmós kikloforías*
nurse	η νοσοκόμα	*i nosokóma*
nutmeg	το μοσχοκάρυδο	*to moschokáridho*

O

object	το αντικείμενο	*to andikímeno*
occupied/taken	κατειλημμένος	*katiliménos*
October	ο Οκτώβριος	*o októvrios*
odometer	το κοντέρ	*o kontér*
off (of meat)	χαλασμένος	*chalazménos*
offer	προσφέρω	*prosféro*
office	το γραφείο	*to ghrafío*
oil	το λάδι	*to ládhi*
oil level	η στάθμη του λαδιού	*i státhmi too ladhyóo*
ointment	η αλοιφή	*i alifí*
ointment for burns	η αλοιφή για εγκαύματα	*i alifí ya engkávmata*
OK	εντάξει	*endáxi*
old	μεγάλος	*meghálos*
olive oil	το ελαιόλαδο	*eleóladho*
olives	οι ελιές	*i elyés*
omelette	η ομελέτα	*i oméleta*
on	πάνω σε	*páno se*
on board ship	στο πλοίο	*sto plío*
once	μια φορά	*mya forá*
oneway traffic	μονόδρομος	*monódhromos*
onion	το κρεμμύδι	*to kremídhi*
open	ανοιχτός	*anichtós*
open (verb)	ανοίγω	*anígho*
opera	η όπερα	*i ópera*
operate	εγχειρίζω	*engchirízo*
operator (telephone)	η τηλεφωνήτρια	*i tilefonítria*
operetta	η οπερέτα	*i operéta*
opposite	απέναντι	*apénandi*
opposite to	αντίκρυ σε	*andíkri se*
optician	ο οπτικός	*o optikós*
orange	το πορτοκάλι	*to portokáli*
orange juice	ο χυμός πορτοκαλιού	*o himós portokalyóo*
orange (colored)	πορτοκαλής	*portokalís*
orchestra (theater)	η πλατεία	*i platía*
order (noun, e.g. a meal)	η παραγγελία	*i parangelía*
order (verb, e.g. a meal)	παραγγέλνω	*parangélno*
others	άλλοι	*áli*
out of order	χαλασμένος	*chalazménos*
outside	έξω	*éxo*
overnight duty	η διανυκτέρευση	*i dhianiktérefsi*
overpass	η οδογέφυρα	*i odhoyéfira*
oysters	τα στρείδια	*ta strídhya*

15

P

packed lunch	το πακέτο του μεσημεριανού φαγητού	to pakéto too mesimeryanóo fayitóo
pacifier	η πιπίλα	i pipíla
page	η σελίδα	i selídha
pain	ο πόνος	o pónos
pain-killer	το παυσίπονο	to pafsípono
paint	η μπογιά	i boyá
painting (art of)	η ζωγραφική	i zoghrafikí
painting (object)	ο πίνακας	o pínakas
palace	το παλάτι	to paláti
pan	η κατσαρόλα	i katsaróla
pane of glass	το τζάμι	to dzámi
panty liner	η μικρή πετσέτα υγείας	i mikrí petséta iyías
paper	το χαρτί	to chartí
paraffin oil	το πετρέλαιο	to petréleo
parasol	η ομπρέλα	i ombréla
parcel	το δέμα	to dhéma
pardon	συγγνώμη	signómi
parents	οι γονείς	i ghonís
park (verb)	παρκάρω	parkáro
park	το πάρκο	to párko
parliament (building)	η βουλή	i voolí
parsley	ο μαϊντανός	o maidanós
partner	ο/η σύζυγος	o/i sízighos
party	το πάρτυ	to párti
pass (road)	προσπερνάω	prospernáo
passable (road or stream)	βατός	vatós
passenger	ο επιβάτης	o epivátis
passport	διαβατήριο	to dhiavatíryo
passport photograph	η φωτογραφία διαβατηρίου	i fotoghrafía dhiavatiríoo
patient	ο ασθενής	o asthenís
pavement	το πεζοδρόμιο	to pezodhrómio
pay the bill	πληρώνω	pliróno
pay (verb)	πληρώνω	pliróno
pea	ο αρακάς	o arakás
peach	το ροδάκινο	to rodhákino
peanuts	τα φιστίκια	ta fistíkya
pear	το αχλάδι	to achládhi
pedestrian crossing	η διάβαση πεζών	i dhiávasi pezón
pedicure	το πεντικιούρ	to pedikyóor
pen	το στυλό	to stiló
pencil	το μολύβι	to molívi
penis	το πέος	to péos
pension	η σύνταξη	i síndaxi
pepper	το πιπέρι	to pipéri
pepper (vegetable)	η πιπεριά	i piperyá
performance	η παράσταση	i parástasi
perfume	το άρωμα	to ároma
perm (verb)	κάνω περμανάντ	káno permanánt
perm (hair)	η περμανάντ	i permanánt
permit	η άδεια	i ádhya
person	το άτομο	to átomo
personal	προσωπικός	prosopikós
pets	τα κατοικίδια ζώα	ta kaitkídhia zóa
pharmacy	το φαρμακείο	to farmakío

15

phone	το τηλέφωνο	to tiléfono
phone (verb)	τηλεφωνώ	tilefonó
phone book	ο τηλεφωνικός κατάλογος	o tilefonikós katáloghos
phone booth	ο τηλεφωνικός θάλαμος	o tilefonikós thálamos
phone number	ο αριθμός	o arithmós
photocopier	το φωτοτυπικό μηχάνημα	to fototipikó michánima
photocopy (verb)	κάνω φωτοαντίγραφο	káno photandígrafo
photocopy	το φωτοαντίγραφο	to photandígrafo
photograph	η φωτογραφία	i fotohrafía
pick up	παίρνω	pérno
picnic	το πικνίκ	to pikník
pier	η προκυμαία	i prokiméa
pigeon	το περιστέρι	to peristéri
pill	το χάπι	to chápi
pillow	το μαξιλάρι	to maxilári
pillowcase	η μαξιλαροθήκη	i maxilarothíki
pin	η καρφίτσα	i karfítsa
pineapple	ο ανανάς	o ananás
pipe	η πίπα	i pípa
pipe tobacco	ο καπνός για την πίπα	o kapnós ya timbípa
pity	κρίμα	kríma
place of entertainment	το κέντρο	to kéndro
place	ο τόπος	o tópos
place of interest	το αξιοθέατο	to axiothéato
plan	το σχέδιο	to schédhyo
plant	το φυτό	to fitó
plastic	πλαστικός	plastikós
plastic bag	η σακούλα	i sakóola
plate	το πιάτο	to pyáto
platform	η πλατφόρμα, η γραμμή	i platfórma, i ghramí
play	το θεατρικό έργο	to theatrikó érgho
play (verb)	παίζω	pézo
playground	η παιδική χαρά	i pedhikí chará
playing cards	τα χαρτιά	ta chartyá
pleasant	ευχάριστος	efcháristos
please	παρακαλώ	parakaló
pleasure	η απόλαυση	i apólafsi
pleasure (it's a)	χαίρω πολύ	héro polí
pleasure, with	ευχαρίστως	efcháristos
plum	το δαμάσκηνο	to dhamáskino
pocket knife	ο σουγιάς	o sooyás
point	δείχνω	dhíchno
poison	το δηλητήριο	to dhilitírio
police court	το αυτόφωρο	to aftóforo
police	η αστυνομία	i astinomía
police station	το αστυνομικό τμήμα	to astinomikó tmíma
policeman	ο αστυνομικός	o astinomikós
pond	η λιμνούλα	i limnóola
pony	το πόνυ	to póni
pop concert	η συναυλία ποπ	i sinavlía pop
population	ο πληθυσμός	o plithizmós
pork	το χοιρινό κρέας	to hirinó kréas
port	το λιμάνι	to limáni

Word list

15

porter (doorman)	ο θυρωρός	o thirorós
porter	ο αχθοφόρος	o achthofóros
portion	η μερίδα	i merídha
post (zip) code	ο ταχυδρομικός κώδικας	o tahidhromikós kódhikas
post office	το ταχυδρομείο	to tahidhromío
postcard	η καρτ-ποστάλ	i kartpostál
postal charges	τα ταχυδρομικά τέλη	ta tahidhromiká téli
potato	η πατάτα	i patáta
potato chips	τα τσιπς	ta tsips

R

refrigerator	το ψυγείο	to psiyío
region	η περιοχή	i periohí
registered	συστημένος	sistiménos
registration number	ο αριθμός κυκλοφορίας	o arithmós kikloforías
reliable	αξιόπιστος	axiópistos
religion	η θρησκεία	i thriskía
religion	η πίστη	i písti
rent out	νοικιάζω	nikyázo
repair (verb)	επιδιορθώνω	epidhiorthóno
repairs	η επιδιόρθωση	i epidhiórthosi
repeat	επαναλαμβάνω	epanalamváno
reserve	κλείνω	klíno
reserved	κρατημένος	kratiménos
responsible	υπεύθυνος	ipéfthinos
rest	ξεκουράζομαι	xekoorázome
restaurant	το εστιατόριο	to estiatório
retired	συνταξιούχος	sintaxióochos
return (ticket)	μετ' επιστροφής	metepistrofís
reverse	κάνω όπισθεν	káno ópisthen
rheumatism	ο ρευματισμός	o revmatizmós
rice	το ρύζι	to rízi
riding (horseback)	η ιππασία	i ipasía
riding school	η σχολή ιππασίας	i scholí ipasías
right of way	η προτεραιότητα	i protereótita
right	δεξιά	dhexyá
right, on the	δεξιά	dhexyá
ripe	ώριμος	órimos
river	το ποτάμι	to potámi
road service	ΕΛΠΑ	i elpá
road suitable for cars	ο αυτοκινητόδρομος	o aftokinitódhromos
roasted	ψημένος	psiménos
rock	ο βράχος	o vráchos
roll (bread)	το ψωμάκι	to psomáki
roof (flat)	η ταράτσα	i tarátsa
roof rack	η σχάρα αυτοκινήτου	i schára aftokinítoo
room service	η εξυπηρέτηση δωματίου	i exipirétisi dhomatíoo
room number	ο αριθμός δωματίου	o arithmós dhomatíoo
room	το δωμάτιο	to dhomátyo
rope	το σκοινί	to skiní
rosé wine	κρασί ροζέ	krasí rozé
rotary	η ροτόντα	i rotónda
route	η πορεία	i poría
rowboat	η βάρκα	i várka
rubber	το λάστιχο	to lásticho

rubber band	το λαστιχάκι	to lasticháki
rucksack	το σακίδιο	to sakídhyo
rude	αγενής	ayenís
ruins	τα ερείπια	ta erípya
run into	συναντώ	sinandó

S

sad	θλιμμένος	thliménos
safe	ασφαλής	asfalís
safe (deposit box)	το χρηματοκιβώτιο	to chrimatokivótyo
safety pin	η παραμάνα	i paramána
sail	αρμενίζω	armenízo
sailboat	το ιστιοφόρο	to istiofóro
salad oil	το λάδι	to ládhi
salad	η σαλάτα	i saláta
salami	το σαλάμι	to salámi
sale	το ξεπούλημα	to xepóolima
salt	το αλάτι	to aláti
same	ο ίδιος	o ídhyos
sandy beach	η πλαζ	i plaz
sanitary pad	η πετσέτα υγείας	i petséta iyías
sardines	οι σαρδέλες	i sardhéles
satisfied	πολύ ευχαριστημένος/η	polí efcharistiménos/i
Saturday	το Σάββατο	to sávato
sauce	η σάλτσα	i sáltsa
sauna	η σάουνα	i sáoona
sausage	το λουκάνικο	to lookániko
savory	πικάντικος	pikándikos
say	λέγω	légho
scarf	το κασκόλ	to kaskól
scenic walk	η βόλτα	i vólta
school	το σχολείο	to scholío
scissors	το ψαλίδι	to psalídhi
scooter	η βεσπα	i véspa
scorpion	ο σκορπιός	o skorpyós
Scotland	η Σκωτία	i skotía
scrambled eggs	η στραπατσάδα	i strapatsádha
screw	η βίδα	i vídha
screwdriver	το κατσαβιδι	to katsavídhi
sculpture	η γλυπτική	i ghliptikí
sea	η θάλασσα	i thálasa
search	ψάχνω	psáchno
search for	ψάχνω	psáchno
seasickness	η ναυτία	i naftía
seat	η θέση	i thési
seatbelt	η ζώνη	i zóni
second	δεύτερος	dhéfteros
second (of time)	το δευτερόλεπτο	to dhefterólepto
secondhand	μεταχειρισμένος	metahirizménos
secretion	η έκκριση	i ékrisi
sedative	το ηρεμιστικό	to iremistikó
see	βλέπω	vlépo
self timer (photo)	ο αυτορρυθμιζόμενος φωτοφράκτης	o aftorithmizómenos fotofráktis
semi-skimmed	ημίπαχο	imípacho
send	στέλνω	stélno
sentence	η πρόταση	i prótasi

September	ο Σεπτέμβριος	o septémvrios
serious	σοβαρός	sovarós
service	η εξυπηρέτηση	i exipirétisi
shade	ο ίσκιος	o ískyos
shallow	ρηχός	richós
shampoo	το σαμπουάν	to sampwán
shark	ο καρχαρίας	o karcharías
shave (verb)	ξυρίζω	xirízo
shaver	η ξυριστική μηχανή	i xiristikí michaní
shaving brush	το πινέλο ξυρίσματος	to pinélo xirízmatos
shaving cream	η κρέμα ξυρίσματος	i kréma xirízmatos
shaving soap	το σαπούνι ξυρίσματος	to sapóoni xirízmatos
sheet	το σεντόνι	to sendóni
sherry	το σέρυ	to séri
shirt	το πουκάμισο	to pookámiso
shoe	το παπούτσι	to papóotsi
shoe shop	το υποδηματοπωλείο,	to ipodhimatopolío, to
	το παπουτσάδικο	papootstádhiko
shoe polish	το βερνίκι παπουτσιών	to verníki papootsyón
shoelace	το κορδόνι	to kordhóni
shop	το μαγαζί	to maghazí
shop	ψωνίζω	psonízo
shop assistant	η πωλήτρια	i polítria
shop window	η βιτρίνα	i vitrína
shopping center	το εμπορικό κέντρο	to emborikó kéndro
short	κοντός	kondós
short circuit	το βραχυκύκλωμα	to vrachikíkloma
shortly	σε λίγο	se lígho
shoulder	ο ώμος	o ómos
show	η παράσταση	i parástasi
shower	το ντους	to doos
shutter	το παντζούρι	to padzóori
sick	άρρωστος	árostos
side of the street	η μεριά του δρόμου	i meryá too dhrómoo
sieve	το σουρωτήρι	to soorotíri
sign (verb)	υπογράφω	ipoghráfo
sign	η πινακίδα	i pinakídha
signature	η υπογραφή	i ipoghrafí
silence	η ησυχία	i isihía
silver	το ασήμι	to asími
silver-plated	επάργυρος	epáryiros
simple	απλός	aplós
single	μονός	monós
single (ticket)	απλό εισιτήριο	apló isitírio
single (unmarried)	ανύπανδρος	anípandhros
sister	η αδερφή	i adherfí
sit	κάθομαι	káthome
size	το νούμερο	to nóomero
skating	το πατινάζ	to patináz
skin	το δέρμα	to dhérma
skin rash	το εξάνθημα	to exánthima
skirt	η φούστα	i fóosta
sleep	κοιμάμαι	kimáme
sleeping pills	τα υπνωτικά	ta ipnotiká
sleeping car	το βαγκον-λί	to vagonlí
slides	τα σλάιτς	ta sláidz
slip (woman's)	το μεσοφόρι	to mesofóri

Word list

15

slow train	το αργό τρένο	to arghó tréno
small	μικρός	mikrós
small change	τα ψιλά	ta psilá
smell of (verb)	βρομώ	vromó
smoke	ο καπνός	o kapnós
smoke (verb)	καπνίζω	kapnízo
smoked	καπνιστός	kapnistós
smoking compartment	το βαγόνι καπνίσματος	to vaghóni kapnízmatos
snake	το φίδι	to fídhi
snorkel	ο αναπνευστήρας	o anapnevstíras
snow	το χιόνι	to hyóni
snowing, it is	χιονίζει	hyonízi
soap powder	η σαπουνόσκονη	i sapoonóskoni
soap	το σαπούνι	to sapóoni
soap dish	η σαπουνιέρα	i sapoonyéra
soccer	το ποδόσφαιρο	to podhósfero
soccer match	ο ποδοσφαιρικός αγώνας	o podhosferikós aghónas
socket	η πρίζα	i príza
socks	οι κάλτσες	i káltses
soft drink	το αναψυκτικό	to anapsiktikó
soft toy	το ζωάκι (παιδιού)	to zoáki (pedhyóo)
sole	η σόλα	i sóla
sole (fish)	η γλώσσα	i ghlósa
someone	κάποιος	kápyos
sometimes	μερικές φορές	merikés forés
somewhere	κάπου	kápoo
son	ο γιος	o yos
soon	γρήγορα	ghríghora
sore throat	ο πονόλαιμος	o ponólemos
sorry	λυπάμαι	lipáme
sort/type	το είδος	to ídhos
soup	η σούπα	i sóopa
sour	ξινός	xinós
source	η πηγή	i piyí
south wind	ο νοτιάς	o notyás
souvenir	το σουβενίρ	to soovenír
spaghetti	τα μακαρόνια	ta makarónya
spare	η ρεζέρβα	i rezérva
spare	το ανταλλακτικό	to andalaktikó
spare parts	τα εξαρτήματα ρεζέρβας	ta exartímata rezérvas
spare tire	η ρεζέρβα	i rezérva
spare wheel	η ρόδα ρεζέρβα	i ródha rezérva
speak	μιλάω	miláo
special	εξαιρετικός	exeretikós
specialist	ο ειδικός	o idhikós
speciality	η σπεσιαλιτέ	i spesialité
speed limit	η ανώτατη ταχύτητα	i anótati tahítita
spell	συλλαβίζω	silavízo
spicy	πικάντικος	pikándikos
splinter	η αγκίδα	angídha
spoon	το κουτάλι	to kootáli
sport	ο αθλητισμός	o athlitizmós
sports center	το αθλητικό κέντρο	to athlitikó kéndro
sportsground	το γήπεδο	to yípedho
sprain	στραμπουλίζω	stramboolízo

Word list

15

spring	η άνοιξη	i ánixi
square	η πλατεία	i platía
square (shape)	το τετράγωνο	to tetrághono
square meter	το τετραγωνικό μέτρο	to tetraghonikó métro
squeeze (verb)	ζουλώ	zooló
stain	ο λεκές	o lekés
stairs	η σκάλα	i skála
stamp	το γραμματόσημο	to ghramatósimo
start	παίρνω μπρος	pérno bros
station	ο σταθμός	o stathmós
statue	το άγαλμα	to ághalma
sty	η διαμονή	i dhiamoní
stay (verb)	μένω	méno
steal	κλέβω	klévo
steel	το ατσάλι	to atsáli
stench	η μπόχα	i bócha
sting (verb)	τσιμπάω	tsimbáo
stitch (verb)	ράβω	rávo
stitches (medical)	τα ράμματα	ta rámata
stockings	οι κάλτσες	i káltses
stomach	το στομάχι	to stomáchi
stomach cramp	η κράμπα στην κοιλιά	i krámpa stingilía
stomachache	ο στομαχόπονος	o stomachóponos
stools (medical)	τα κόπρανα	ta kóprana
stop	σταματάω	stamatáo
stop	η στάση	i stási
stopover	η ενδιάμεση προσγείωση	i endhiámesi prosyíosi
storm, there is a	έχει τρικυμία	ehí trikimía
storm	η θύελλα	i thíela
straight ahead	ίσια	ísya
straight hair	ίσια μαλλιά	ísya malyá
straw	το καλαμάκι	to kalamáki
strawberries	οι φράουλες	i fráooles
street	ο δρόμος, η οδός	o dhrómos, i odhós
strike	η απεργία	i aperyía
stroll around town	η βόλτα στην πόλη	i vólta stimbóli
strong	δυνατός	dhinatós
study	σπουδάζω	spoodházo
stuffing	η γέμιση	i yémisi
subtitled	με υπότιτλους	me ipotítloos
subway	το μετρό	to metró
subway station	ο σταθμός του μετρό	o stathmós too metró
succeed	τα καταφέρνω	ta kataférno
sugar	η ζάχαρη	i záchari
sugar cubes	οι κύβοι ζάχαρης	i kívi zácharis
suit	το κοστούμι	to kostóomi
suitcase	η βαλίτσα	i valítsa
summer time	η καλοκαιρινή ώρα	i kalokyeriní óra
summer	το καλοκαίρι	to kalokyéri
sun hat	το καπέλο ηλίου	to kapélo ilíoo
sun	ο ήλιος	o ílyos
sunbathing	η ηλιοθεραπεία	i ilyotherapía
Sunday	η Κυριακή	i kiryakí
sunglasses	τα μαύρα γυαλιά	ta mávra yalyá
sunrise	η ανατολή	i anatolí
sunset	το ηλιοβασίλεμα	to ilyovasílema

sunstroke	η ηλίαση	i ilíasi
suntan lotion	η κρέμα ηλίου	i kréma ilíoo
suntan oil	το λάδι ηλίου	to ládhi ilíoo
supermarket	η υπεραγορά	i iperaghorá
surcharge	το συμπληρωματικό ποσόν	to simpliromatikó posón
surf board	η σανίδα του σερφ	i sanídha too serf
surfing	το σέρφιγκ	to sérfing
surname	το επώνυμο	to epónimo
surprise	η έκπληξη	i ékplixi
swallow (verb)	καταπίνω	katapíno
swamp	το τέλμα	to télma
sweat	ο ιδρώτας	o idhrótas
sweater	το πουλόβερ	o poolóver
sweet	γλυκός	ghlikós
sweet corn	το καλαμπόκι	to kalambóki
swim (verb)	κολυμπώ	kolimbó
swimming costume	το μαγιό	to mayó
swimming pool	η πισίνα	i pisína
swindle	η απάτη	i apáti
switch	ο διακόπτης	o dhiakóptis
synagogue	η συναγωγή	i sinaghoyí
syrup	το σιρόπι	to sirópi

T

table	το τραπέζι	to trapézi
table tennis	το πιγκ πογκ	to ping pong
tablet	το χάπι	to chápi
take (photograph)	βγάζω	vgházo
take	παίρνω	pérno
take (verb, of time)	διαρκώ/κρατώ	dhiarkó/krató
take pictures	φωτογραφίζω	fotoghrafízo
talcum powder	το ταλκ	to talk
talk	μιλάω	miláo
talk to (intimately)	ψωνίζω κάποιον	psonízo kápyon
tampon	το ταμπόν	to tampón
tap	η βρύση	i vrísi
tap water	το νερό της βρύσης	to neró tis vrísis
taste	δοκιμάζω	dhokimázo
tasty	νόστιμος	nóstimos
tax-free shop	το μαγαζί αφορολόγητων ειδών	to maghazí aforolóyiton idhón
taxi	το ταξί	to taxí
taxi stand	η στάση ταξί	i stási taxí
teaspoon	το κουταλάκι	to kootaláki
tea	το τσάι	to tsái
teapot	η τσαγιέρα	i tsayéra
tee shirt	η φανέλα	i fanéla
telegram	το τηλεγράφημα	to tileghráfima
telephone number	ο αριθμός τηλεφώνου	o arithmós tilefónoo
telephone receiver	το ακουστικό	to akoostikó
telescopic lens	ο τηλεφακός	o tilefakós
television	η τηλεόραση	i tileórasi
telex	το τηλέτυπο	to tilétipo
temperature	η θερμοκρασία	i thermokrasía
temporary filling	το προσωρινό σφράγγισμα	to prosorinó sfráyizma

temporary	προσωρινός	*prosorinós*
tender	μαλακός	*malakós*
tennis	το τένις	*to ténis*
tennis ball	η μπάλα του τένις	*i bála too ténis*
tennis court	το γήπεδο τένις	*to yípedho ténis*
tennis racket	η ρακέτα του τένις	*i rakéta too ténis*
tent	η σκηνή	*i skiní*
tent peg	το πασαλάκι της σκηνής	*to pasaláki tis skinís*
terrible	φοβερός	*foverós*
thank you	ευχαριστώ	*efcharistó*
thank (verb)	ευχαριστώ	*efcharistó*
thaw	λιώνω	*lióno*
the same	το ίδιο	*to ídhyo*
theater	το θέατρο	*to théatro*
theft	η κλοπή	*i klopí*
there	εκεί	*ekí*
thermometer	το θερμόμετρο	*to thermómetro*
thick	χοντρός	*chondrós*
thief	ο κλέφτης	*o kléftis*
thigh	το μπούτι	*to bóoti*
thin	λεπτός, αδύνατος	*leptós, adhínatos*
things	τα πράματα	*ta prámata*
think (verb)	νομίζω	*nomízo*
third	το τρίτο	*to tríto*
thirst	η δίψα	*i dhípsa*
this afternoon	σήμερα το απόγευμα	*símera to apóyevma*
this evening	απόψε	*apópse*
this morning	σήμερα το πρωί	*símera to proí*
thread	η κλωστούλα, η κλωστή	*i klostóola, i klostí*
throat	ο λαιμός	*o lemós*
throat lozenges	οι παστίλιες για το λαιμό	*i pastílyes ya to lemó*
throw up (be sick)	κάνω εμετό	*káno emetó*
thunderstorm	η καταιγίδα	*i kateyídha*
Thursday	η Πέμπτη	*i pémpti*
ticket	το εισιτήριο	*to isitírio*
tidy up (verb)	μαζεύω	*mazévo*
tie	η γραβάτα	*i ghraváta*
tights	το καλτσόν	*to kaltsón*
time	η ώρα	*i óra*
times	φορές	*forés*
timetable	το δρομολόγιο	*to dhromolóyo*
tip	το πουρμπουάρ	*to poorbwáar*
tire	το εξωτερικό λάστιχο	*to exoterikó lásticho*
tire lever	ο μοχλός για την αφαίρεση λάστιχων	*o mochlós ya tin aféresi lástichon*
tire pressure	η πίεση λάστιχων	*i píesi lástichon*
tissues	τα χαρτομάντηλα	*ta chartomándila*
to let	νοικιάζεται	*nikyázete*
toast (French-style)	η φρυγανιά	*i frighanyá*
tobacco	ο καπνός	*o kapnós*
tobacco (loose)	ο καπνός	*o kapnós*
tobacco shop	το καπνοπωλείο	*to kapnopolío*
today	σήμερα	*símera*
toe	το δάχτυλο	*to dháchtilo*

together	μαζί	*mazí*
toilet	η τουαλέτα	*i twaléta*
toilet paper	το χαρτί υγείας	*to chartí iyías*
toiletries	τα είδη τουαλέτας	*ta ídhi twalétas*
tomato	η ντομάτα	*i domáta*
tomato puree	ο ντοματοπολτός	*o domatopoltós*
tomato sauce	το κέτσαπ	*to kétsap*
tomorrow	αύριο	*ávrio*
tongue	η γλώσσα	*i ghlósa*
tonic water	το τόνικ	*to tónik*
tonight	απόψε	*apópse*
too	επίσης	*epísis*
tooth	το δόντι	*to dhóndi*
toothache	ο πονόδοντος	*o ponódhondos*
toothbrush	η οδοντόβουρτσα	*i odhondóvoortsa*
toothpaste	η οδοντόπαστα	*i odhondópasta*
toothpick	η οδοντογλυφίδα	*i odhondoghlifídha*
torch	ο φακός	*o fakós*
total	το σύνολο	*to sínolo*
tough	σκληρός	*sklirós*
tour guide	ο ξεναγός	*o xenaghós*
tour boat	το εκδρομικό καραβάκι	*to ekdhromikó karaváki*
tourist card	η τουριστική κάρτα	*tooristikí kárta*
tourist class	η τουριστική θέση	*i tooristikí thési*
tourist menu	το τουριστικό μενού	*to tooristikó menóo*
Tourist Information Office	το τουριστικό γραφείο	*to tooristikó ghrafío*
tow rope	το σκοινί τραβήγματος	*to skiní travíghmatos*
tow	τραβάω	*traváo*
towel	η πετσέτα	*i petséta*
tower	ο πύργος	*o pírghos*
town hall	το δημαρχείο	*to dhimarchío*
toys	τα παιχνίδια	*ta pechnídhya*
traffic	η κυκλοφορία	*i kikloforía*
traffic light	το φανάρι	*to fanári*
trailer	το τροχόσπιτο	*to trochóspito*
train ticket	το εισιτήριο τρένου	*to isitírio trénoo*
train	το τρένο	*to tréno*
trainers	τα παπούτσια αθλητισμού	*ta papóotsya athlitizmóo*
translate	μεταφράζω	*metafrázo*
travel agent	το πρακτορείο ταξιδίων	*to praktorío taxidhíon*
travel	ταξιδεύω	*taxidhévo*
traveler	ο ταξιδιώτης	*taxidhyótis*
traveler's check	η ταξιδιωτική επιταγή	*i taxidhyotikí epitayí*
treatment	η θεραπεία	*i therapía*
triangle	το τρίγωνο	*to tríghono*
trim (verb)	ψαλιδίζω	*psalidhízo*
trip	το ταξίδι	*to taxídhi*
trousers	το παντελόνι	*to pandelóni*
trout	η πέστροφα	*i péstrofa*
truck	το καμιόνι	*to kamyóni*
try on	δοκιμάζω	*dhokimázo*
tube	το σωληνάριο	*to solinário*
Tuesday	η Τρίτη	*i tríti*
tumble drier	το στεγνωτήριο	*to steghnotírio*

Word list

15

tuna	ο τόννος	o tónos
tunnel	το τούνελ	to tóonel
TV guide	ο οδηγός ραδιοφώνου/ τηλεόρασης	o odhighós radhiofónoo/tileórasis
tweezers	το τσιμπιδάκι	to tsimbidháki

U

ugly	άσχημος	áschimos
ulcer	το έλκος	to élkos
umbrella	η ομπρέλα	i ombréla
under	κάτω από	káto apó
underground train system	το δίκτυο του μετρό	to dhíktio too metró
underpants (ladies')	το σλιπάκι	to slipáki
underpants	το σώβρακο	to sóvrako
understand	καταλαβαίνω	katalavéno
underwear	τα εσώρουχα	ta esóroocha
undress	γδύνω	ghdhíno
unemployed	άνεργος	ánerghos
uneven	άνισος	ánisos
university	το πανεπιστήμιο	to panepistímio
unleaded	αμόλυβδος	amólivdhos
urgency	η βιασύνη	i viasíni
urgent	επείγον	epíghon
urine	τα ούρα	to óora
use (verb)	χρησιμοποιώ	chrisimopyó
usually	συνήθως	siníthos
utensil (cooking)	το σκεύος	to skévos

V

vacate	αδειάζω	adhyázo
vaccinate	εμβολιάζω	emvolyázo
vagina	ο κόλπος	o kólpos
vaginal infection	η κολπική μόλυνση	i kolpikí mólinsi
valid	έγκυρος	éngkiros
valley	η κοιλάδα, το λαγκάδι	i kiládha, to langádhi
valuable	πολύτιμος	polítimos
van	το φορτηγάκι	to fortigháki
vanilla	η βανίλια	i vanílya
vase	το βάζο	to vázo
vaseline	η βαζελίνη	i vazelíni
veal	το μοσχαρίσιο κρέας	to moscharísyo kréas
vegetable soup	η χορτόσουπα	i chortósoopa
vegetables	τα λαχανικά	ta lachaniká
vegetarian	ο χορτοφάγος	o chortofághos
vein	η φλέβα	i fléva
venereal disease	το αφροδίσιο νόσημα	to afrodhísyo nósima
vest	η φανέλλα	i fanéla
via	μέσω	méso
video camera	η κινηματογραφική μηχανή	i kinimatoghrafikí michaní
video recorder	το βίντεο	to vídeo
videotape	η βιντεοταινία	i videotenía
view	η θέα	i théa
village	το χωριό	to choryó
village festival/fair	το πανηγύρι	to paniyíri
village woman	η χωριάτισσα	i choriátisa

Word list

15

viral infection	η ίωση	i íosi
visa	η βίζα	i víza
visit	η επίσκεψη	i epískepsi
visit (verb)	επισκέπτομαι	episképtome
visiting time	η ώρα επίσκεψης	i óra episképsis
vitamin pills	τα χάπια βιταμίνης	ta chápya vitamínis
vitamin	η βιταμίνη	i vitamíni
volcano	το ηφαίστειο	to iféstio
volleyball	το βόλλεϋ	to vólei
vomit	κάνω εμετό	káno emetó

W

wait for	περιμένω	periméno
waiter	το γκαρσόνι	to garsóni
waiting room	η αίθουσα αναμονής	i éthoosa anamonís
waitress	η σερβιτόρα	i servitóra
wake up	ξυπνάω	xipnáo
Wales	η Ουαλλία	i walia
walk	ο περίπατος	o perípatos
walk (verb)	περπατώ	perpató
wallet	το πορτοφόλι	to portofóli
wardrobe	η γκαρντ-ρόμπα	i gard-róba
warm	θερμός, ζεστός	thermós, zestós
warn	προειδοποιώ	proidhopió
warning	η προειδοποίηση	i proidhopíisi
wash	πλένω	pléno
washing machine	το πλυντήριο	to plindírio
washing	η μπουγάδα	i booghádha
wasp	η σφήκα	i sfíka
water	το νερό	to neró
waterski	το θαλάσσιο σκι	to thalásio ski
waterfall	ο καταρράχτης	o kataráchtis
waterproof	αδιάβροχος	adhiávrochos
wave pool	πισίνα με κύματα	pisína me kímata
waves	τα κύματα	ta kímata
way (road)	ο δρόμος	o dhrómos
way	η κατεύθυνση	i katéthinsi
way, on the	στο δρόμο	sto dhrómo
we	εμείς	emís
weak	αδύνατος	adhínatos
weather	ο καιρός	o kyerós
weather forecast	το μετεωρολογικό δελτίο	to meteoroloyikó dheltío
wedding	ο γάμος	o ghámos
Wednesday	η Τετάρτη	i tétarti
week	η εβδομάδα	i evdhomádha
weekend	το σαββατοκύριακο	to savatokíryakoadh
weekly ticket	η εβδομαδιαία κάρτα	evdhomiéa kárta
welcome	καλώς ήρθατε	kalós írthate
well	καλά	kalá
well	καλός	kalós
well done (cooking)	καλοψημένος	kalopsiménos
west (to the)	δυτικά	dhitiká
wet	υγρός	ighrós
wetsuit	το κοστούμι του σερφ	to kostóomi too serf
what?	τί;	ti?
wheel	η ρόδα	i ródha

wheelchair	το καροτσάκι (αναπήρων)	to karotsáki (anapíron)
when?	πότε;	póte?
where?	πού;	poo?
which?	ποιός;	pyos?
whipped cream	η σαντιγί	i santiyí
white	άσπρος	áspros
who?	ποιός;	pyos?
why?	γιατί;	yatí?
wide-angle lens	ο ευρυγώνιος φακός	o evrighónyos fakós
widow	η χήρα	i híra
widower	ο χήρος	o híros
wife	η γυναίκα	i yinéka
wind	ο άνεμος	o ánemos
windbreak	ο ανεμοφράκτης	o anemofráchtis
window	το παράθυρο	to paráthiro
window (booking office, bank)	η θυρίδα	i thirídha
wine	το κρασί	to krasí
wine list	ο κατάλογος κρασιών	o katáloghos krasyón
winter	ο χειμώνας	o himónas
witness	ο μάρτυρας	o mártiras
woman	η γυναίκα	i yinéka
wonderful	θαυμάσιος	thavmásios
wood	το ξύλο	to xílo
wool	το μαλλί	to malí
word	η λέξη	i léxi
work	η δουλειά	dhoolyiá
working day	η εργάσιμη ημέρα	i erghásimi méra
workout	η άσκηση	i áskisi
worn	τριμμένος	triménos
worried	ανήσυχος	anísichos
wound	η πληγή	i pliyí
wrap	τυλίγω	tilígho
wrench	το γαλλικό κλειδί	to ghalikó klidhí
wrist	ο καρπός	o karpós
write	γράφω	ghráfo
write down	καταγράφω	kataghráfo
writing paper	το χαρτί αλληλογραφίας	to chartí aliloghrafías
written document	γραπτά	ghraptá
wrong	λάθος	láthos

Y

yacht	το γιωτ	to yot
year	ο χρόνος	o chrónos
yellow	κίτρινος	kítrinos
yes	ναι	ne
yesterday	χτες	chtes
yogurt	το γιαούρτι	to yaóorti
you	εσείς	esís
youth hostel	ο ξενώνας νεότητας	o xenónas neótitas

Z

zipper	το φερμουάρ	to fermwár
zoo	ο ζωολογικός κήπος	o zo-oloyikós kípos
zucchini	το κολοκυθάκι	to kolokitháki

Word list

15

Basic grammar

1 The Greek alphabet

(See also 1.8 Telephone alphabet)

α	A	álfa	somewhere between **a** in **car** and **u** in **cup**
ß	B	víta	as **v** in **van**
γ	Γ	gháma	as **y** in **yet** before **e** and **i** sounds; before any other sound, a hard **g** (as in **grab**) as far down your throat as possible. (This sound is shown as **gh** in the transcriptions.)
δ	Δ	dhélta	as hard **th** in **this**
ε	E	épsilon	as **e** in **met**
ζ	Z	zíta	as **z** in **zoo**
η	H	íta	as **i** in **quarantine** (i.e. like the **ee** in **feet**)
θ	Θ	thíta	as soft **th** in **thin**
ι	I	yóta	as **i** in **quarantine** (i.e. like **ee** in **feet**), but before another vowel often becomes **y**- as in **yacht**)
κ	K	kápa	as **k** in **kitchen**, but before **e**- and **i**-sounds, more like **ky**)
λ	Λ	lámdha	as **l** in **lick**
μ	M	mi	as **m** in **mat**
ν	N	ni	as **n** in **not**
ξ	Ξ	xi	as **x** in **box**
o	O	ómikron	as **o** in **pop**
π	Π	pi	as **p** in **pin**
ρ	P	ro	closer to a Scottish **r** than an English one
σ,ς	Σ	síghma	like a soft English **s** as in **sit**, except before the sounds **b,gh,dh** and **m**, when it is like **z**
τ	T	taf	as **t** in **tin**
υ	Y	ípsilon	as **i** in **quarantine** (i.e. like the **ee** in **feet**)
φ	Φ	fi	as **f** in **fit**
χ	X	hi	as **h** in **hat** before **i** or **e** sounds; before any other sound, as Scottish **ch** in **loch**
ψ	Ψ	psi	as combination of **p** and **s** in **tops**
ω	Ω	omégha	as **o** in **pop**

2 Vowels

There are only five vowels sounds in Greek, approximating to the English sounds a (see α), e (see ε), ee (see ι), o (see o) and oo as in foot (spelt ou), but several of these sounds can be written in a number of ways:

ε, αι both = **e** in **met**
η, ι, υ, ει, οι = **i** in **quarantine** (ie. like **ee** in **feet**)
o, ω = o in pot
N.B. αυ and ευ are pronounced **av** and **ev** before ß, γ, δ, ζ, λ, μ, ν, ρ, τ or another vowel; before anything else they are pronounced **f**. Thus **αυγό** (egg) is pronounced *avghó* but **απόλαυση** (enjoyment) is pronounced *apólafsi*.

3 The consonant combinations

As well as the single consonant sounds indicated above in the description of the alphabet, there are a number of sounds which can only be written with two consonants together. These are:

b   as in **bet** = μπ
d   as in **dog** = ντ
g   as in **gap** = γκ.

Similarly, when one word ends in the sound n and the next begins with the sound p, t, or k the following changes occur:

τον πατέρα (ton patéra - the father) becomes *tombatéra*
την ταβέρνα (tin tavérna - the taverna) becomes *tindavrna*
τον κατ¨ογο (ton katálogho) becomes *tongatálogho*.

The following combinations of consonants also make particular sounds:

γγ = **ng** as in **sing**
γξ = **n(g)x** – somewhere between **things** and **thinks**
γχ = **n(g)ch** – try pronouncing the middle of **melancholy** with a Scotish **ch** after the **n**. Fortunately, the last two combinations are relatively rare!

4 Stress and accents

The accents on Greek words indicate where the stress goes. In the pronunciation guide the stresses are also marked with an accent, e.g. **o πατέρας** = *o patéras*. The vowel **ou** is transcribed as **oo** when not stressed and **óo** when stressed.
N.B. Any two other vowels together in the transcription must be pronounced separately, e.g. **αεροδρόμιο** must be pronounced *a-e-rodhrómyo*.

5 Nouns

Greek nouns each have a gender, which can be masculine, feminine or neuter. They also have endings which change to show whether they are singular or plural, and whether they are nominative, accusative or genetive case. The nominative case is always used for the subject of an action; the accusative is used for the direct object of an action and after most prepositions (in, to, for etc.); the genetive is used to show possession (of someone or something) or indirect objects (to someone or something).

The most common forms are as follows:

masculine nouns have a singular nominative ending in:	**-ος,-ας** or **-ης**
a corresponding plural nominative endings in:	**-οι -ες -ες**
feminine nouns have a singular nominative ending in:	**-η** or **-α**
a plural nominative ending in:	**-ες**
neuter nouns have a singular nominative ending in:	**-ο, -ι,** or **-α**
a corresponding plural nominative ending in:	**-α, -ια -ατα**

In a brief introduction to Greek grammar it is not possible to give all the details of all the categories of nouns. Here are three common nouns in all the cases of both singular and plural, with the definite article (the):

	masculine singular	masculine plural
nominative (subject case)	**ο δρόμος** (the road)	**οι δρόμοι**
accusative (direct object case)	**τον δρόμο**	**τους δρόμους**
genetive (indirect object case)	**του δρόμου**	**των δρόμων**

	feminine singular	feminine plural
nominative (subject case)	**η γυναίκα** (woman)	**οι γυναίκες**
accusative (direct object case)	**τη(ν) γυναίκα**	**τις γυναίκες**
genetive (indirect object case)	**της γυναίκας**	**των γυναίκων**

	neuter singular	neuter plural
nominative (subject case)	**το παιδί** (child)	**τα παιδιά**
accusative (direct object case)	**το παιδί**	**τα παιδιά**
genetive (indirect object case)	**του παιδιού**	**ού των παιδιών**

N.B. Like nouns the definite article (the) also has, as can be seen from the above examples, three genders and nine cases. It must always agree with its noun in number, gender and case. Christian names, names of countries, days of the week and months all take a definite article in front of them, eg. **ο Γιάννης** (John), **η Αγγλία** (England), **η Παρασκευή** (Friday), **ο Μάιος** (May).

6 Adjectives

Adjectives in Greek behave like the definite article: they agree in gender, number and case with the noun which they describe. The most common form of adjective has endings which are similar to those of the nouns:

	masc. singular	fem. singular	neut. singular
nominative (subject case)	**-ος**	**-α/-η**	**-ο**
accusative (direct object case)	**-ο**	**-α/-η**	**-ο**
genetive (indirect object case)	**-ου**	**-ας/-ης**	**-ου**
	masc. plural	fem. plural	neut. plural
nominative (subject case)	**-οι**	**-ες**	**-α**
accusative (direct object case)	**-ους**	**-ες**	**-α**
genetive (indirect object case)	**-ων**	**-ων**	**-ων**

Adjectives usually stand before their noun, as in English.

The words **αυτός** (this) and **εκείνος** (that) also function as adjectives, but they stand before the definite article. So this beautiful house and of that beautiful woman in Greek are: **αυτό το ωραίο σπίτι** and **εκείνος της ωραίας γυναίκας.**

7 Verbs

Verbs in Greece are very complex. They are made up of two parts: the stem, which gives the main idea of the verb (eg. have, want, drink), and the ending, which shows whether the action is singular or plural, first, second or third person, and past or present. So in the verb **πληρώνω** (pay), the stem is **πληρών-** (the idea of payment) and the ending **-ω** shows that the action is first person singular and present tense. There are two stems for most verbs, and also different sets of endings for active and passive. It is obviously not possible to give more than very basic information in a brief introduction like this. Below is the present tense (active) of the verbs **έχω** (have) and **Θέλω** (want), divided up to show the standard endings.

I have	**έχ-ω**	(écho)	I want	**Θέλ-ω**	(thélo)
You have	**έχ-εις**	(éhis)	You want	**Θέλ-εις**	(thélis)
He/she/it has	**έχ-ει**	(éhi)	He/she/it wants	**Θέλ-ει**	(théli)
We have	**έχ-ουμε**	(échoome)	We want	**Θέλ-ουμε**	(théloome)
You have	**έχ-ετε**	(éhete)	You want	**Θέλ-ετε**	(thélete)
They have	**έχ-ουν**	(échoon)	They want	**Θέλ-ουν**	(théloon)

8 Personal pronouns

As we have seen no separate word for I, you, we etc. is necessary to show the subject of an action, as the ending of the verb gives you this information. The object forms of the personal pronoun are as follows: me = **με**, you (sing.) = **σε**, him = **τον**, her = **τη**, it = **τον, τη** or **το** (according to the gender) we = **μας**, you (plur.) = **σας**, they = **τους** (for people) or **τους** or **τα** (for things). These forms stand before the verb, eg. **το Θέλω** (I want it). To say my, your, his etc., use the following forms after the noun: my = **μου**, your (sing.) = **σου**, his = **του**, her = **της**, our = **μας**, your (plur.) = **σας**, their = **τους** (for people and things): eg. **τα παιδιά μας** = our children.

9 Prepositions

The most common prepositions are **για** (for), **από** (from) and **σε** (in or to). They are all followed by the accusative case, eg. **από την Αθήνα** (from Athens), **για τον φίλο μου** (for my friend). The preposition **σε** contracts with the definite article in the following ways: **σε+τον = στον, σε+την = στην, σε+το = στο,** eg. **στο Λονδίνο** (in London).